STALAG XXA

AND THE ENFORCED MARCH FROM POLAND

STALAG XXA

AND THE ENFORCED MARCH FROM POLAND

STEPHEN WYNN

Pen & Sword

MILITARY

AN IMPRINT OF PEN & SWORD BOOKS LTD.
YORKSHIRE - PHILADELPHIA

First published in Great Britain in 2020 by
PEN AND SWORD MILITARY
An imprint of
Pen & Sword Books Limited
Yorkshire – Philadelphia

ISBN 978 1 52675 446 2

Typeset in Times New Roman 11.5/14 by
SJmagic DESIGN SERVICES, India.
Printed and bound in the UK by TJ Books Ltd.

Pen & Sword Books Limited incorporates the imprints of Atlas, Archaeology,
Aviation, Discovery, Family History, Fiction, History, Maritime, Military, Military
Classics, Politics, Select, Transport, True Crime, Air World, Frontline Publishing,
Leo Cooper, Remember When, Seaforth Publishing, The Praetorian Press,
Wharncliffe Local History, Wharncliffe Transport, Wharncliffe True Crime and
White Owl.

For a complete list of Pen & Sword titles please contact
PEN & SWORD BOOKS LIMITED
47 Church Street, Barnsley, South Yorkshire S70 2AS, United Kingdom
E-mail: enquiries@pen-and-sword.co.uk
Website: www.pen-and-sword.co.uk

Or
PEN AND SWORD BOOKS
1950 Lawrence Rd, Havertown, PA 19083, USA
E-mail: Uspen-and-sword@casematepublishers.com
Website: www.penandswordbooks.com

Contents

Introduction

Torun is a city in the northern central region of Poland, and sits on the banks of the famous Vistula River. It has a long history which can be traced as far back as the eighth century. Over the centuries Torun has seen many changes, including being part of both Prussia and Germany.

It is universally accepted as being one of the most beautiful cities in Europe, with its medieval district having been designated a UNESCO World Heritage Site in 1997. By the beginning of 2019, the city had a population of more than 200,000.

During the Second World War, however, Torun was known for a totally different reason due to the fifteen existing defensive artillery forts which surround the city. Collectively they were used as a German prisoner of war camp known as Stalag XXA, and held prisoners from a variety of Allied nations. At its peak, the camp catered for some 20,000 men.

The camps first wartime inhabitants were Polish soldiers captured after their surrender at the Battle of Westerplatte, the first battle of the war in Europe after the German invasion of Poland. The battle lasted for seven days between 1 and 7 September 1939, and resulted in some 200 Polish soldiers being captured and taken prisoner.

Although this book is based on the diary of Leonard J. Parker, and covers the period of 19 January to 21 April 1945, it also looks at those who were prisoners there, how they came to be there, and the reasons behind why they were forced to leave in January 1945. While many ultimately survived their ordeal, there were many others who did not, having succumbed to the extreme conditions they had to endure on that enforced march in the harsh Polish winter of 1945.

Chapter One

Prisoners of Stalag XXA

The first British prisoners of war who found themselves incarcerated at Stalag XXA were 400 men who had been captured as a result of the Allied campaign in Norway, between 9 April and 10 June 1940. The next group of Allied soldiers to be held as prisoners at Torun were some 4,500 who were captured at Dunkirk at the end of May 1940, before they could make good their escape on the flotilla of ships sent across the English Channel to rescue them.

On 12 June 1940, the Scottish 51st (Highland) Infantry Division, which not surprisingly was made up of a number of Scottish regiments, including the Argyll and Sutherland Highlanders, the Gordon Highlanders, and the Seaforth Highlanders, surrendered to the Germans at Saint-Valery-en-Caux, just thirty minutes after the French had done the same thing.

The 51st and their French counterparts had been trying to make their way down the coast to Le Harve to be evacuated, but the Germans reached the coast at Saint-Valery-en-Caux, cutting off their proposed route and forcing them back in to the town. When the main body of the Highland Division was forced to surrender, the British commander, Major-General Victor Morven Fortune, became one of the highest ranking officers in the British Army to be captured by the Germans throughout the entire war. Along with Fortune, some 10,000 officers and men of the 51st Highland Infantry Division were captured at St Valery-en-Caux and marched off to spend the rest of the war in captivity.

Although they didn't know it at the time, their destination was to be the German prisoner of war camp of Stalag XXA at Torun, situated about 120 miles north west of Warsaw. From St Valery they were marched across France to Germany via Belgium. Some of the prisoners had the comparative luxury of being transported in canal barges, but to get to their final destination, the last leg of the journey was made by train in the back of cattle trucks.

During that long and arduous journey, some 134 members of the 51st Highland Infantry Division not only managed to escape, but they also made it all the way back home to England. Before the war was over, the 51st Highland Infantry Division had been involved in the action in North Africa, during the 2nd Battle of El Alamein in August 1942, the Tunisia campaign of April 1943, and D-Day.

As more and more Allied prisoners of war were sent to Torun, so more of the artillery forts were needed as accommodation for them. The nationalities of those who arrived at the camp varied, which was a reflection of the military strength of the Germans, and their ability to rapidly overrun and defeat the Allied nations they had invaded. In no time at all the camp at Torun included Polish, French, Belgium, Norwegian, Australian and Yugoslavian soldiers. As a result of German successes during Operation Barbarossa, Soviet prisoners of war began arriving at Torun from June 1940. Captured members of the RAF who had been shot down over German-occupied Europe, were housed separately from other Allied prisoners of war.

The Germans put 'other ranks' prisoners at Torun to work as per the Geneva Convention. For most, this meant working as part of 'labour units', or *Arbeitskommando*, most of whom were then hired out to either military or civilian contractors.

The location in northern Poland was a safe place to locate such a camp as far as the Germans were concerned; it was too far away from the Allies' front lines for them to be able to mount any rescue attempts. That was on the assumption, however, that Operation Barbarossa, the invasion of the Soviet Union, was going to be successful; it wasn't.

With matters not going according to plan in the Soviet Union, German military authorities decided they needed to move all Allied prisoners of war held in captivity in northern Poland, to prevent them from being rescued by the now quickly advancing Soviet troops, thereby providing the Allies with a ready-made army that could almost immediately be put back in to a war-like unit, once again ready and able to fight against them.

Soldiers of the Soviet Red Army finally liberated the camp on 1 February 1945. Among the number of British prisoners of war held at Torun throughout the course of the war were men from all walks of life, from different backgrounds, social classes, religious beliefs and political persuasions. Men who, if hadn't been for the war, would probably have never met or associated with each other.

One such individual worth a mention is George Frank McLardy, who was born in Waterloo, Lancashire, in 1915. He was a very bright young man and excelled both in the sporting arena and in academia. In 1934 when he left school, he continued his education by studying at the Liverpool School of Pharmacy. After successfully completing a five-year course in pharmacy, he qualified as a Member of the Pharmaceutical Society in October 1939. That same year had also seen him join the British Union of Fascists, which was a fascist political party set up by Oswald Moseley in 1932. The party was banned by the British government in 1940, even though by then its once large following had long since dwindled, due in the main to its Nazi-style stance against the Jews. But the authorities were genuinely concerned that the party's remaining hardcore followers might form a pro-Nazi 'fifth-column'. To make this possibility even less likely, many of the remaining members of the British Union of Fascists were interned under emergency wartime powers, brought in at the beginning of the war. McLardy was not one of them. Even though his activities had been monitored by MI5 since 1937, he was still allowed to enlist in the British Army at the outbreak of the war when he volunteered for the Royal Army Medical Corps.

Due to his qualification as a pharmacist, he was quickly promoted to the rank of sergeant, and on 9 May 1940, despite the British Expeditionary Force being in full retreat and heading as speedily as it could towards the French coast and the English Channel, McLardy found himself arriving in France. His unit had only made it as far as Brussels, before they too were forced back towards the French coast at Dunkirk. On 31 May 1940, and with the evacuations at Dunkirk already well underway, McLardy was captured in the northern French town of Wormhout. There is an element of confusion surrounding his capture as it is believed that he was on his own and not with the rest of his unit when he was taken as a prisoner of war by the Germans. Initially he was sent to Stalag XXA prisoner of war camp at Thorn in Poland, and from there he was sent to Stalag XXl-A, which was located at Schildberg, also in Poland. He spent the following three years at Schildberg utilising his medical knowledge in the camp's hospital, doing the best that he could for his fellow comrades.

In September 1943, McLardy was moved again, this time to Stalag XXl-D at Posen, which was reputedly the worst camp in the whole of Poland. Not looking forward to another harsh Polish winter,

McLardy approached one of the German *Abwehr* or intelligence officers who were stationed at Schildberg, and informed him that he wanted to apply to join the Waffen-SS. The somewhat surprised *Abwehr* officer translated McLardy's handwritten application from English into German, typed it up and forwarded it to Berlin. Three weeks later he found himself being escorted to Berlin by an *Abwehr* guard. He was actually taken to Stalag lllD/517S at Genshagen, just south of Berlin. This was a camp which had been built by the Germans in 1943, with the specific intention of tempting Allied soldiers who were sent there to betray their own countries.

While at Genshagen, McLardy met a number of like-minded Allied prisoners of war. One was Lance Corporal William Charles Brittain of the Royal Warwickshire Regiment, who was captured in Crete in June of 1941 while serving with No. 4 Commando. Brittain allowed himself to become a member of 'staff' at Genshagen, and later a *Rottenfhurer* in the Waffen-SS. Even though by changing sides he had effectively become a traitor, he returned to the UK after the war in 1946; court-martialled at Colchester, he was sentenced to only ten years imprisonment, but released on compassionate grounds just two months later, having being diagnosed with an incurable disease.

Another was Roy Nicholas Courlander, an Englishman serving in the New Zealand Army, having only arrived in New Zealand in 1938. Because of his knowledge of both German and French he ended up serving in New Zealand's Intelligence Corps. He was sent out to Greece, where he was captured by the Germans on 29 April 1941 and sent to a prisoner of war camp at Maribor in Yugoslavia, where he acted as an interpreter.

Courlander's was a somewhat unusual story. Although initially a member of the British Free Corps, he volunteered for service with the German war correspondent unit, *SS-Standarte Kurt Eggers* on the Western Front, but along with another member of the British Free Corps, he boarded a train and made his way to Brussels in Belgium, where he arrived on 3 September 1944. Once there, the two men linked up with members of the Belgium resistance, with whom they fought against the Germans. He was wounded during the fighting and gave himself up to British forces the following day.

On his return to England, Courlander faced a court martial, was found guilty and sentenced to fifteen years imprisonment for assisting the enemy, a sentence which was later reduced to nine years on appeal; he was actually released on 2 October 1951, after having served just six years in prison.

Edwin Barnard Martin, a Canadian from Ontario, was a private in the Canadian Army's Essex Scottish Regiment, and was captured on the now famous Dieppe raid, which took place in August 1942.

After the war he faced a court martial before Canadian authorities, for being a member of the British Free Corps and for being an informer for the Germans; Martin was sentenced to twenty-five years imprisonment.

Alfred Minchin was a seaman in the British Merchant Navy, serving on board SS *Empire Ranger*, part of a convoy en route to Murmansk in Russia when it was sunk by German bombers off the coast of Norway on 28 March 1942. Minchin survived the attack, was picked up by a German destroyer and taken as a prisoner of war. He later joined the British Free Corps; in fact, it is said that it was he who came up with the name.

At the end of the war he was captured, brought back to Britain and tried at the Central Criminal Court of the Old Bailey, to answer a charge of conspiring to assist the enemy, which was an offence under the Defence Regulations. He was found guilty and sentenced to seven years penal servitude.

The Royal Army Medical Corps and Army Dental Corps records office, situated at Colet Court, Hammersmith, London, show a Sergeant 7522956 F.G. McLardy, who was held as a prisoner of war at Stalag lll-D in Berlin. His PoW number was 12948.

McLardy was made an *SS-Unterscharfuhrer* and put in charge of propaganda for the British Free Corps. His main job became travelling around Germany and visiting prisoner of war camps where British soldiers were held. He would hand out leaflets about the British Free Corps, while making wild claims of how successful and large the organisation was. His lies and half-truths were blatant. He told likely recruits that the corps already had two divisions. During the Second World War, an infantry division could range anywhere between 8,000 and 30,000 men. He even claimed that one of the divisions came under the command of senior British officers, was backed by the British government, and was already fighting against the Russians.

The Germans were obviously expecting great things of the British Free Corps, partly because they hoped that the hundreds of disillusioned British soldiers being held in German captivity would enlist. They went as far as having nearly 1,000 special uniforms made up that included a collar patch with three lions on it, along with a Union Jack patch on one of the sleeves, together with an armband that said 'British Free Corps', written in gothic German script. The Corps were moved to a former monastery at Hildesheim, a city in Lower Saxony, which had become an SS barracks

McLardy gave his new recruits lectures in such areas as Bolshevism, the German Language and Economics. It quickly became clear to most of the new recruits that McLardy had simply spun them a yarn, for which they had fallen and accepted without question. Some of the new recruits remained in the Corps, not out of any desire to follow Nazi ideology, or a misplaced loyalty to Adolf Hitler, but because it was an easy alternative to PoW camp life. Remaining where they were provided them with beer and alcohol, along with the ability to fraternise with local German women.

McLardy seemed to sense that the war was coming to an end, and so at the end of August 1944, fed up with the in-fighting between himself and the other main Free Corps protagonists, he volunteered for service with the Waffen-SS medical corps, or *Sanitatswesen*.

He eventually surrendered to American forces in the German village of Dohren, in Saxony-Anhalt, and was handed over to the British on 19 April 1945. After the war he was returned to the UK, where he was court martialled for voluntarily aiding the enemy while a prisoner of war. On 1 January 1946, at the Blacon Camp near Chester, he was sentenced to life imprisonment, which was later commuted to fifteen years imprisonment. In 1953, having served just seven years, mostly at HMP Parkhurst on the Isle of White, he was released, whereupon he emigrated to Germany and worked as a pharmacist, having earned a degree in chemistry from Cambridge University while in prison. He married a German woman with whom he had two sons.

Chapter Two

Some PoWs who died at Stalag XXA

The following is a list of British prisoners of war who died while in captivity at Stalag XXA, throughout the course of 1940. Initially they were buried in the local Torun cemetery and then exhumed after the war, with most being moved to Malbork cemetery in Poland after the war.

Basted/Rasted, John. 2 November 1940.

Bosko, John.

Bowerman, Hedley James. Private 5674325, 22 years of age and served with the 1st Battalion, Oxford and Bucks Light Infantry, died on 25 August 1940.

Cooper, Leonard. Gunner 1059918, 37 years of age and served with the 2nd Battery, 1st Searchlight Regiment, Royal Artillery, died on 22 October 1940.

Coutts, Robert Baird. Driver T/76608, 31 years of age and served with the Royal Army Service Corps, died on 20 August 1940.

Dann, Edward William. Private 1020138, 34 years of age and served with the Gordon Highlanders, but was attached to Royal Army Ordnance Corps, died on 22 August 1940.

Ford, George Edgar. Private 5111743, 20 years of age and served with the 7th Battalion, Royal Warwickshire Regiment, died on 9 September 1940.

Garden, Edward C. Private 2877210, 25 years of age and served with the 1st Battalion, Gordon Highlanders, died on 22 July 1940.

Godfrey, Frank Victor Cyril. Private 6286959, who was 19 years of age and served with the 5th Battalion, The Buffs (Royal East Kent Regiment). Died on 1 July 1940.

Griffiths, Leonard Earle. Private 6345169, who was 29 years of age and served with the 7th Battalion, Queens Own Royal West Kent Regiment, died on 22 August 1940

Hall, Elias. Private 2819332, 27 years of age and served with the 2nd Battalion, Seaforth Highlanders, died on 16 August 1940.

Kember, William Benjamin. Driver T/109411, 28 years of age and served with the Royal Army Ordnance Corps, died on 7 July 1940.

Kyle, Alexander. Sergeant 7884687, 23 years of age and served with the 15th/19th The King's Royal Hussars, Royal Armoured Division, died on 27 August 1940.

Murrant, Arthur. Private 6344555, 19 years of age and served with the 1st Battalion, Queens Own Royal West Kent Regiment, died on 2 August 1940.

McKay, Peter. Private 2823943, 22 years of age and served with the Seaforth Highlanders, died on 8 August 1940.

Pickering, Fred. Private 6283896 who was 34 years of age and served with the 2nd Battalion, The Buffs (Royal East Kent Regiment), died on 22 August 1940.

Race, Thomas Henry. Trooper 558409, 20 years of age and served with the 15th/19th The Kings Royal Hussars, Royal Armoured Corps, died on 30 September 1940.

Rattray, Robert. Driver 85981, 20 years of age and served with the Royal Army Service Corps, died on 6 September 1940.

Redpath, James Samuel Laing. Signalman 2580531, 22 years of age and served with the 51st Divisional Signals, Royal Corps of Signals, died on 27 September 1940.

Robinson, John.

Russell, James. Fusilier 4271570, 20 years of age and served with the 7th Battalion, Royal Northumberland Fusiliers, died on 2 November 1940.

Smith, Robert. Private 7622867, 23 years of age and served with the Royal Army Ordnance Corps, died on 18 July 1940.

Stout, John Christopher. Private 4444371, 35 years of age and served with the 11th Battalion, Durham Light Infantry, died on 2 November 1940.

Sykes, Herbert. Private 5668740, 33 years of age and served with the 2nd/5th Battalion, The Queens Royal Regiment (West Surrey), died on 21 July 1940.

Weatherston, William. Private 3055335, 21 years of age and served with the 1st Battalion, Royal Scots, died on 2 August 1940. Has no known grave but his name is commemorated on the Dunkirk Memorial.

Winchester, William Alfred. Sergeant 6343870, 24 years of age and served with the 4th Battalion, Queens Own Royal West Kent Regiment, died on 15 July 1940.

Wooding, William Henry. Private 5106850, 26 years of age and served with the 7th Battalion, Royal Warwickshire Regiment, died on 7 September 1940.

Allied prisoners of war who died while in captivity at Stalag XXA during the course of the Second World War were either buried in the garrison military cemetery in Torun, or at Malbork Commonwealth War Cemetery, even though the latter was some 120 kilometres north of Torun.

The burials at Malbork Commonwealth War Cemetery are mostly of Allied prisoners of war who died while being held at the nearby camps. Stalag XXB, which was in Malbork; Stalag lA, situated at Stablack, which can be found between Malbork and Gdansk; Stalag 2A at Starogard, a few kilometres south of Stablack; and Stalag XXA, at Torun (Thorn), which was about 120 kilometres south of Malbork. When the war finished and hostilities ceased, the graves service of the British Army of the Rhine moved all the graves from the local burial grounds to Malbork cemetery, together with other Commonwealth graves in outlying places in areas where their permanent maintenance could not be assured. The largest number came from Torun. The cemetery contains 226 Second World War burials.

Chapter Three

Germany Crumbles

The Red Army crossed the Danube on 29 November 1944 and General Patton's Third Army crossed the River Saar on 5 December 1944. The Battle of the Bulge began with a counter-attack in the Ardennes on 16 December, while elements of the German SS massacred seventy-one captured American prisoners of war at Malmedy in Belgium on 17 December 1944. Prisoners of war who were held in work camps in the Konigsberg area of Germany were evacuated on 24 December 1944. When Europe was divided up by the Allies after the war, Koningsberg became the Russian city of Kalliningrad.

On 12 January 1945, the Red Army launched its offensive into German-occupied Poland, with the city of Warsaw falling just five days later on 17 January. Two days after that, on 19 January, Allied prisoners of war being held at Stalag Luft VII, at Bankau, are evacuated in blizzard conditions, followed by those held at Stalag 344 at Lamsdorf on 22 January 1945, and moved westwards.

While tens of thousands of prisoners of war who were spread across Germany pondered an uncertain future, news of the marches had reached home. In Britain, those who knew that their sons, husbands or sweethearts were being held in camps in Poland and parts of Germany, had seen the news of the Russian military advances and were no doubt looking forward to having their loved ones back home again.

On 22 January 1945 the War Office in London issued a press release which had been approved by Prime Minister Winston Churchill himself. But it really wasn't what most people wanted to hear. It simply said, 'So far the War Office has received no information of the release of any British and Commonwealth prisoners-of-war by the advancing Red Army. An announcement will be made as soon as reliable information is available.' The announcement continued:

It is known that the German Authorities have been moving
to the west prisoners of war and civilians from camps which
are likely to be overrun. It should be appreciated that in the
present conditions in Germany it might be some time before
details of these transfers reach London.

On 27 January 1945, as the Russians crossed the River Oder, some forty
miles from Sagan, where they discovered the horrors of Auschwitz;
all the prisoners at Stalag Luft III were evacuated from the camp and
marched, in atrocious weather conditions, to Stromburg. There, they
were placed in cattle trucks and taken to a town called Tormstat where
they were held in what had previously been a Merchant Navy camp
at Mevleg-Milag. It was almost, but not quite, a case of out of frying
pan into the flames. Although liberated from their incarceration by
the Germans, they were not free men, far from it. They remained at
Mevleg-Milag until April 1945 and were then marched towards Lubeck.
The Red Army crossed the German border on 31 January 1945.

On 6 February 1945, Stalag Luft IV at Gross Tychow was evacuated
of its remaining prisoners, who then had to endure an eighty-six-day
march west, in advance of the Russian Army. That really doesn't sound
like the actions of a liberating nation. But it has long since been believed
that the Russians were actually holding on to as many Allied prisoners of
war as possible, just in case things didn't quite go their way in a political
sense from the meetings that were taking place between America,
Britain and Russia. For Stalin in particular, not somebody who trusted
either Churchill or Roosevelt, it made sense for him to hold on to Allied
prisoners of war until he was absolutely certain, that in the aftermath
of the war, he wouldn't find himself embroiled in a new war against
America and Britain.

On 9 February 1945, British and American troops swept through
Germany's Siegfreid Line, with the intention of taking as much of
Germany as they could. After all, if it was in their hands, it wouldn't fall
in to the hands of the Russians.

On 23 February 1945, American forces finally crossed the Ruhr. Just
five days later, and with the Germans desperate to escape the rapidly
advancing Red Army, it is estimated that some 2 million German civilians
and soldiers fled the Russians through the Baltic port of Danzig.

On 7 March 1945, American forces again crossed the Rhine, this time south of Cologne. This resulted in Hitler issuing his 'Nero Order' on 19 March, for the destruction of any and all industry, transport and agriculture that would likely fall in to the hands of the Allies. Just five days later, on 24 March, Germany's position worsened even further, when both American and British forces crossed the Rhine in force across a wide front.

Chapter Four

The Diary of Leonard J. Parker –
Part One: January 1945

Sometime in 2017 a diary came in to my possession, that had been written by a Leonard J. Parker, a prisoner of war who had been held by the Germans at their camp at Torun. He had entitled it *A Diary of Liberation*, and it covered the period between 19 January and 21 April 1945; it was a record of his personal experience of an enforced march between Torun and eventual freedom at Odessa, and his forward journey back home to his family.

To make absolutely certain I had the right man, I checked the British Prisoners of War lists that covered the Second World War. Records show that there are 261 men with the surname Parker, who at one time or another had been captured and held as a prisoner of war by the Germans. The diary shows that the enforced march began from camp Stalag XXA, in Thorn, which is just one of the ways Torun was spelt. The second stop on the march was at a town named Kopernikus.

There was only one L.J. Parker on the British Prisoners of War list. He was a Private (6097195) in The Buffs (Royal East Kent Regiment). His prisoner of war number was 28795, and he was shown as having been a prisoner at camp number 344, in Lambinowice, in Poland. The same list also recorded an L. Parker who was in the Royal Air Force, service number 1039027, but it does not record his rank. He was a prisoner at camp 357, and the reason I mention him is because the camp was located at Kopernikus, Poland. His prisoner of war number was 3423.

I believe that out of the two men, it is L.J. Parker whose diary I have. All Royal Air Force personnel were kept together in one camp, whereas soldiers from all different regiments were placed in the same camp. On the first page of the diary, which I will come to shortly, L.J. Parker makes reference to Sammy Kydd who, after the war, became a well-known and much-loved actor who appeared in hundreds of films and numerous TV series. Kidd was an infantry soldier and served with the Queen Victoria Rifles as part of the British Expeditionary Force in France, but was captured soon after his arrival, and sent to the Torun prisoner of war camp in what was then German-occupied western Poland. He was in captivity for the rest of the war, all of it at Stalag XXA, where he was in charge of the camp's theatrical productions. Many years later he wrote his autobiography entitled *For You The War Is Over*, which included his experiences as a prisoner of war at Torun.

On arrival at Torun the captured Allies were first registered as prisoners of war. This was immediately followed by their fingerprints and photograph being taken. Each man was then issued with a small metal tag which was worn on a piece of string round the neck. Similar to a soldier's own ID tag, it was perforated down the middle with each half including the camp number along with the prisoner's individual prison number. This was so that if a man died, one half of the tag remained with the body and the other half was sent to the authorities of the nation from where the man came.

To say that the accommodation was basic was an understatement, remembering of course that the camp consisted of a number of old military forts. There was not much in the way of light that found its way in, as many of the rooms had only a single small window. For most they did not even have a bed to sleep in, there was just a layer of straw covering the floor for men to get comfortable in. Most of the forts suffered with dampness and had water running down the inner walls, which during the winter made it nigh on impossible to keep warm. Some prisoners were billeted in tents in the grounds of the fort, which had the advantage of being able to allow more light in and not have to contend with water running down the walls, but the bedding was still only straw.

The food rations ensured that nobody ever put on weight. The daily diet consisted of one meal a day, usually served at lunch time and consisted of potato soup, which had a distinct lack of actual potato, and a loaf of black bread. The bread had to be shared between up to six men, and came with a miniscule amount of margarine.

Torun was one of the main camps to which Germany also sent her prisoners in the early days of the war. Once men had been registered, they were sent out to one of the numerous Working Camps as part of a working detail.

Although illness in the camp wasn't rampant it did exist. Malnutrition affected many, due to a combination of the size of the food rations and the work that men were required to undertake. The main illness in the camp was dysentery which, because of the conditions and the numbers of men in the camp, was easily transmitted. It is an intestinal infection which can last up to a week and results in diarrhoea that contains blood. Other symptoms include abdominal cramps and tenderness, nausea, vomiting and a temperature of 38°c or higher. Other ailments included diphtheria and scabies, which were not unusual in such conditions.

So this was the background to what British and Allied soldiers left behind when they began their enforced march on 19 January 1945. Here is Leonard's diary in its entirety.

Friday 19 January 1945

Lord, what an effort to get out of bed this morning. It is still extremely cold; all the windows were thickly frosted over and the inside walls of the hut were filmed with a thin coating of ice which quickly turns to running water as soon as the stove is lit and the room warms up a little. As the wash-house is practically a solid block of ice, Sammy Kidd and I, and one or two others now, are still washing in the corner of the room in water left on the stove overnight. Even this does little to make it less of an ordeal to turn out and face another day of this bitter weather.

The thought of a move in this snow and freezing cold is dismaying. Quite obviously, if we are to be marched as a body back in to Germany there will be no indoor accommodation available en-route for such large numbers; rather it will be 'catch-as-catch-can' as in 1940. In this weather it will mean exposure and no little suffering. If only it were summer.

We went off to work in the usual way this morning but when we arrived at Stalag we found the situation far from normal. Everyone was packing furiously, our own work place was strewn with packing cases and gear, and although

15

no one seems to know when it will start or where we shall go, it is obvious that a move is imminent. And I do mean imminent! All these preparations are not being made just for practice.

According to our news the Russians cannot be much more than about seventy-five to eighty kilometres away from Thorn, and must have already over-run Lamdorf, Stalag Vlll-B.

Stalag Vlll-B was a prisoner of war camp ran by the German Army near the small Polish town of Lamsdorf. There had previously been a prisoner of war camp at the same location, during the Franco-Prussian war of 1870–71, as well as during the First World War.

In 1939 it was reopened to house Polish prisoners captured during the invasion of their country by the Germans in September. But as the war continued, Allied soldiers from numerous different countries were held there, including Australia, Belgium, Britain, Canada, France, Greece, Holland, India, Italy, New Zealand, Palestine, Poland, South Africa, Soviet Union, United States and Yugoslavia.

In 1943, Stalag Vlll-B, became Stalag 344, and prisoners were then transferred to Stalag Vlll-C at Sagan, and Stalag Vlll-D, at Treschen, and the newly named Stalag 344, remained as a base camp. In 1943 Stalag Luft lll, which was for Allied pilots and other flight personnel, had become so overcrowded that more than 1,000 of the camp's prisoners were transferred to Stalag Vlll-B, where part of the camp was fenced off to accommodate the new arrivals, and became Stalag Luft Vlll-B.

In January 1945, many of the Allied prisoners of war from Stalag XXA as well as the Stalag Luft and Stalag Vlll camps, were moved westwards, as the Soviet Armies resumed their offensive against the Germans inside their own country.

The Soviet Red Army eventually reached the camps on 17 March 1945, liberating all of the Allied prisoners of war who were still being held. For those who had already began the march westwards towards Germany, there were those who wouldn't make it. Some of them died of exhaustion, while others died of the bitter cold of the Polish winter. Some made it far enough westwards to be rescued by the American Army, while others were liberated by the Russians who, instead of handing them over to the Allied authorities, held on to them – in some cases for several more months. These Allied prisoners became pawns in a bigger picture as the war began drawing to a close, and the Allied nations began the process of sharing out the spoils of victory.

After the war, the Soviets utilised the Lamsdorf camp to house both German civilians, and military personnel.

Back to the diary of Leonard Parker:

> We wonder what has become of the British prisoners of war there? Have they been evacuated or have the Germans left it too late and the Stalag fallen to the Russians? Has not our own move been left rather overlong too? It seems highly probable to us that we shall be overtaken by the advancing Red Army unless Jerry can move us quickly; and surely his roads and railways must be filled to capacity with troops and supplies. I rather fancy it will be foot slogging for us, in which case it will not be possible to remove us back with any great speed.
>
> Personally, I do not feel too highly elated at the thought of being 'liberated' by the Russians. They are such an unknown quantity and there is no way of speaking with them if we do come in to contact. Unless of course, they have liaison officers from British or American units with them in the field. It is far more comforting to think of falling in to the hands of our own people or of the Americans, but unfortunately we are situated on the doorstep of the Russian front, and would have to travel a very long way to contact the Western Allies. However, after nearly five years behind this wire, I guess my home is a good way.
>
> As they were destroying the negatives of the origin prisoner of war identity photographs taken in 1940 for registration, I seized the opportunity of 'lifting' Jack's and my own. It was a pleasant surprise to Jack when I took them round to the Packets Department. Bob Smith was there having come down with the mail party from the camp; he was eager to have his own 'photo and Mac', so I promised to try to get them. Back I went and with some trepidation and a watchful eye on the Jerry i/c [in charge] I was able to locate the rolls containing these, took them out and nipped

round to the packets once more where we cut off the ones we wanted and burned the rest. These will surely make unique souvenirs.

In the midst of all this activity, at about 1030 this morning, the air raid syrens [*sic*] sounded off, and for the first time it was the real thing. Within a few minutes five Russian planes appeared overhead, flying low and unimpeded by any German fighters. They were trim, fast looking craft of great interest to us being the first of the new vintage we have seen. They had great big red stars on their fuselage and wings and were certainly unlike any we had ever seen before. I expect aeroplanes and weapons have changed almost beyond recognition since we were active at Dunkirk time.

It must have been a strange situation for Leonard and his colleagues to witness, because the weapons, aircraft, ships, tanks, and submarines had improved drastically over the years of the war, and many had certainly changed from what they had been at the outset of the war.

Stalag personnel, both German and Polish were thrown in to a state of confusion bordering on panic, and seemed to have no idea what to do beyond donning steel helmets, rifles and gas masks. All the guards were shouting orders to which no one, least of all the British, paid any attention to at all.

The planes, safely flying past the two lone Anti-Aircraft shells put up, tried to bomb Thorn bridge, but according to later reports they missed it. However they have had a great demoralising effect on the Germans. Things are certainly starting to move now and we are almost hourly expecting to hear artillery in action. This suspense of waiting to move and wondering what the Germans will do about us is a little unnerving.

That must have been a really horrible time for Leonard and his colleagues, because I have no doubt that for some of them 'unnerving' actually meant trepidation, fear and a belief that they would be shot by the Germans rather than allowed to be rescued by the Russians. There was every likelihood that if the German guards felt they were soon going to be overrun and killed by Russian soldiers, they would likely first kill their Allied prisoners either in a blind panic, or in the belief that they would likely turn on them and kill them before the Russians did.

I completed my packing as far as possible tonight and after a hasty meal we four gathered in the bunk for a conference to decide on procedure in the event of a prolonged march. We decided to try to keep together and 'muck in' on whatever came along. Bob has built an ingenious little sled for our kit, as have many others in bland disregard of an order from Debonitz, the Camp Commandant, forbidding them. Why they should be forbidden no one knows. Just contrariness I suppose.

Jack has prepared some emergency haversacks each containing, inter-alia, Bovril, Horlicks, milk powder, chicken essence, tea, sugar, cigarettes and matches; these are to be used only in case of extreme emergency if all other supplies run out or have of necessity to be jettisoned.

Another item worthy of mention here is a small paper Union Jack for each of us which we saved from a supply of Christmas novelties sent out from England. These little flags measure about 2½ by 1½ and it is our intention to wear them conspicuously in our hats so that we shall be readily identifiable as British. We feel that this is the best we can do so that in case we do run in to any Russians they will recognise us as allies. It is all we can do, really, as none of us know any Russian except 'Angelski' which we believe to mean 'English' and 'Tovarich' meaning friend, and we are not really sure about these. Anyway, we shall try to get them in quickly if we meet any itchy-fingered Russkis.

Although the little clock is still ticking away on its shelf and Jack's hurricane lamp burns as brightly as ever, the bunk has assumed a desolate air with all our familiar comforts gone; even the little chairs which Bob made so cleverly from Canadian Red Cross packing cases have been sacrificed to the construction of the sled. Packs, etc., are loaded and waiting to be picked up at a moment's notice. Indeed the whole camp seems somehow unfamiliar and is all on edge just waiting for the word 'Go' which surely cannot be long in coming.

As we four have decided to go it together, we have laid our plans accordingly and have made such preparations as we think best to weather snow and frost in cases of sleeping out, etc. We have also decided to carry coffee and cigarettes for trading on the way. In general we hope to profit from the lessons which we learned so dearly on the 1940 march to the prison camp.

We turned in rather late and despite the talking and activity in the room, I slept like a log.

Saturday 20 January 1945

I was sleeping warmly and soundly when at the ungodly hour of 3 am .... Reveille at the DOUBLE!

Out of bed and finished my packing. Room 37, as ever other in camp, a picture of bustle and scurrying and, as chaps found themselves with too much kit to transport, knee deep in discarded articles of clothing, books, half-emptied tins of Red Cross and the like. Everyone seemed quite calm, Germans excepted and an almost gay, holiday-like atmosphere prevailed. All the chaps were, of all things, highly pleased with the prospect of not having to go to work tomorrow. I expect it was the relief of having something definite at last. The German Camp issued literally hundreds of instructions to us but no one seemed even slightly interested.

After a hurried breakfast, we four met in the bunk, cold and cheerless in the dark and chill of night, and brought the sled and kit out on to the parade ground for loading. The square was already filled with men, equipment and sleds and all the paraphernalia of a move. The air was filled with voices, hundreds of them, some shouting, some talking excitedly, others discussing plans, or just chatting, the whole presenting a strange picture of activity in the darkness lit by innumerable cigarette glows, torches and light streaming from open doors and windows, all black out restrictions completely disregarded.

The Red Cross store was opened and while Mac and I mounted guard over the kit, Jack and Bob drew out our Red Cross food, packed it in to a couple of boxes and brought it back in to the camp where we strapped it on to the sled. As we are 'mucking in' our combined supplies were too much for the sled, so I was given charge of the excess in a little wooden box. I attached a rope to this so I could drag it along like a miniature sleigh as long as the bottom holds out.

Bob's creation looked like a Polar expedition, piled high with kit bags, valises and parcels of Red Cross. All it needed was a dog team to complete the picture. We are well supplied with food and warmly dressed. I had on my battle dress, puttees and stout boots, thick turtle neck sweater, rolled balaclava hat, woollen gloves and greatcoat. Everything was ready.

Reading Leonard Parker's description of their preparation on leaving the camp, painted a detailed picture of life at Stalag XXA, and it certainly didn't come across as a harsh existence at all. His description of drawing food from the Red Cross store as they prepared to leave, made it sound more like a shopping trip to the local supermarket. There was no shortage of military clothing either, which after five years of captivity was somewhat remarkable. However horrendous the march that followed was, Leonard and his colleagues were most definitely as well prepared as they could have possibly been.

Jack and I arranged to march with Bob and Mac, who as Medical Orderlies, were to proceed with the Hospital party. In this way we were assured of keeping together and were able to lend a hand with the sick, many of whom were stretcher cases and could not do anything to help themselves. Those who were too ill to stand a long journey were to be taken to a camp a few miles away, and there left with a skeleton staff to manage as best they could until overtaken by the Russians or until the Germans had driven the Red Army back and were able to reoccupy the evacuated ground.

We felt there was not too much likelihood of the latter happening.

Bob Howard opened his heart and issued 40 cigarettes per man and, although we were fairly well stocked with tobacco, many were not, and would thus be assured of a smoke for a while.

The British Prisoner of War lists for the Second World War show a total of 149 men with the surname of Howard, of these, just seven are shown as having been held captive at Stalag XXA at Torun, but not one of them had the initials of either 'B' or 'R'.

Big Jock disappeared into the cookhouse and reappeared a few minutes later with a little dixie full of hot Oxo so we adjourned for the last time to the bunk to drink it and to have a final look round. Soon, however, loud shouts from outside indicated that things had progressed to the point of moving so we went out and re-joined the column. Before I left the bunk I took down the little cartoon representing 'Big Jock' and 'Farmer Lingane' which had occupied a place of honour since appearance in 'The Camp' and stowed it away carefully in my pocket. If we get through, it will always be a reminder of some good laughs.

The Allied Prisoners of War list for the Second World War shows a Serjeant 834465 J.P. Lingane who served with the Oxfordshire & Buckinghamshire Light Infantry Regiment.

And so finally, about two hours after being hauled out of bed, and to the accompaniment of loud instructions shouted by the guards, to which as ever no one paid any attention, we moved off slowly through the big double gates for the last time and struck off across the fields towards Bromberg. The first leg of our journey from Camp Einheit Drei, Thorn to heaven knows where, had begun.

Bromberg, or 'Bydgoszcz' in Polish, was the site of a wartime massacre. On 3 September 1939, shortly after the Second World War began, the incident referred to as 'Bloody Sunday' took place, resulting in the deaths of both ethnic German and ethnic Polish during the fighting; Nazi propaganda used the deaths of ethnically German Poles and named the incident Bloody Sunday as a pretext for their deadly reprisals against the ethnic Polish people following occupation of the city by German troops on 9 September 1939.

> Some of the home made sleds were no sooner put in motion than they collapsed through overloading and weak construction. The ground, although fairly well covered with snow, was rough and uneven and it proved too much for some of the sleds, especially those built too high and insufficiently supported on their runners. Bob, however, with his usual aptitude, had proven more than equal to the task and had constructed ours low and strong so that, loaded as we were, we were able to get along in fine style. Bob and Jack pulled, Mac pushed: I followed on with my little box bumping along behind. There were many sad scenes of spilled kit and broken sleds to be seen as we pushed on.

The British Prisoner of War list for the Second World War has only two names on it with the name 'Jack'. One of these is a Private 3058405 John (Jack) McDiarmid, of the Seaforth Highlanders, although he is not shown as being a prisoner at Stalag XX. There is also a UK and Allied Prisoners of War list for the Second World War, which has 4,299 names on it, but unfortunately none of them include the prisoner of war camp where the men were held.

> The going was slow, extremely slow of necessity for us because of the sick who could not move above a slow walk and the stretcher cases who were being dragged along or carried laboriously shoulder high. And so our hospital party fell behind the Main body who were soon out of sight.
>
> As we marched along we could see the preparations the Germans had made to try to stem the rushing tide of the Red Army's advance. We made our way through hastily built barricades, over slit-trenches, anti-tank obstacles, and past gun emplacements, machine gun posts and numerous groups

of Jerry soldiers behind their guns at cross-roads and in fields. A remarkable thing I noticed was that there were hundreds and hundreds of yards of trenches, all dug and properly latticed but completely empty. No doubt the Germans had not sufficient troops to man them. Everywhere there hung an ominous air of anticipation and it was strangely quiet. The Germans were not talking to each other, they sat at their posts and looked tense and worried. I suppose they had good reason to be. These oncoming Russians have quite a reputation with Jerry, and not a comforting one. The German propaganda of the last few years, painting the Red Army as a fiend lusting for blood and not particular as to whose blood it was, is now recoiling on to the German soldier. These Huns are scared.

Shortly before we left the open fields and turned in to the main Thorn–Bromberg road, Bob Howard, who was extraordinarily well oiled with '95', pushed his little hand cart out of the column and made his way back towards Thorn followed by 'Norah' Winterbottom. Strangely enough the guards made no effort to stop them, and off they went through the German lines where we lost sight of them as we marched on in the opposite direction. We don't know why they went nor where. It seems a bit risky just yet to be floating around unattached.

We found the main road overflowing with a solid stream of transport vehicles, guns, tanks and marching troops. And they were going in both directions! Here was proof, if proof was needed, of the state of confusion into which the Wehrmacht had been thrown by the concerted attacks on eastern and western fronts. My mind blew back five years to the last time we had been marching along the road as prisoners. We were then being taken into a life of captivity, to be shut behind barbed wire for the rest of the war, for how long no one knew or even dared to guess. And the Germans swept forward, confident, arrogant, victorious. Now what a difference! Here was no conquering Army arrogantly thrusting on, brushing aside all who dared stand in its way; here was no blitzkreig such as we had seen to our cost in 1940. Here rather was a defeated German Army, weakened and exhausted, striking blindly at an enemy who could not be halted; an Army in its death throes. How the mighty had fallen.

None of us felt any too happy at being mixed up with this lot as Russian planes were about and were bound to attack this packed column, and us with it. So we kept as near to the edge as possible, ready at a moments notice to fling ourselves into the comparative shelter of the ditches. Luckily no planes appeared and we arrived at Kopernikus Lager safely, turned off the road and entered the camp. Here we were to leave the sick and re-join the main column.

We found however, that the Main body had already arrived and left some two hours before us and were now well on their way to Bromberg, or should have been. We halted outside the administration buildings of the camp, glad of the rest, while the sick were moved in to the hospital. Here too was confusion and great activity with the Germans working feverishly to get things organised, but not succeeding. Amidst the scene of disorder, shouting and milling around our party stood quite calm and serene, seizing the opportunity to rest, have a bite to eat and a smoke. We waited for the next stage of proceedings.

The difficult circumstances which Leonard and his colleagues found themselves in, were more than likely what saved their lives. With the Russian Red Army rapidly advancing on them from the east, there was not a single German soldier to be found who would have been happy surrendering to the Soviets. However, those same Germans would have been more than happy to surrender to Allied soldiers, towards whom they were marching, in the west. Being captured by the Americans or British, in possession of a large number of Allied prisoners, would have been a strong indicator that they were just guards rather than fanatical, fighting infantry soldiers, prepared to die for the Nazi cause. But if they had killed their captives en route, their atrocities would have quickly been discovered, and their fate would have no doubt been sealed.

A German Lieutenant made several attempts to get us back on to the road and on our way, but our guards were nowhere to be found, having disappeared in to different huts to rest. He could not send us on alone and we paid little attention to his ravings. His attention was soon drawn elsewhere to some British prisoners who had 'borrowed' a small horse-drawn buggy and were busily loading their kit into it. He glared at us, and shouted, 'Very well then. Stay here, damn you!' and stamped off.

Bob had decided to leave his piano accordion here with a friend who was remaining behind to tend to the sick. So away we went in to the British section of the camp. Jack, Mac and I opened a meat roll, cut up a loaf of bread and had our first meal on the road.

By this time however, our guards had been routed out and the column was formed up ready to move off. Bob was still absent, and as we moved slowly back towards the gate and started to follow the Main body's route to Bromberg, he was still missing. Mac was nearly frantic with mingled rage and anxiety and indeed Jack and I too were cursing him roundly for getting separated before we had scarcely begun our trek.

And then the thing that was to shape our whole immediate future happened. Just as we in our turn were about to quit the camp and move off up the road, there came the familiar horrible whine, which although we had not heard since Dunkirk, we recognised at once as artillery shells. And sure enough with a deafening CRUMMP-CRUMMP two shells dropped out on the road only a hundred yards from us, throwing up a shower of earth and rubble and no doubt quite a few assorted pieces of German soldiers as well.

'Back, back in to the camp,' shouted the guards. We certainly didn't need to be told a second time, and about faced and streamed back in to Kopernikus and made our way in to the British section of the camp.

Kopernikus was Stalag 'Kopernikus' at Thorn, which I have referred to in this book as Torun in Poland, about 180 miles northwest of Warsaw. The camp was situated about 1½ miles from Torun railway station from which the prisoners were marched. Later this camp became known as Stalag XXA.

Here we found Bob chatting to his friends, all unaware of what had happened since he left us and of how we had nearly gone off without him.

For an hour or more we stood around in little groups and discussed the situation. The Germans had left us, seemingly to our own devices, and we wondered what was to be our next step. Jack for one, working on the 'out of sight out of mind' principle, was in favour of moving in to the buildings so that we might stand a chance of being left at Kopernikus until liberated by the Russians.

This we finally decided to do, and so we dragged our sleds to the English cookhouse, a brick building on top of a hill. This structure, although exposed and conspicuous, offered many advantages to us in our present position. The roof was plainly marked with Red Crosses, it was the most solidly built place in the camp and it had cellars to which we could retreat in case of air raids.

Jack had many friends on the staff there and after we had moved in to the cook house they invited us down to their billet for a hot meal. Very welcome. Unfortunately however, the camp was packed with Russian prisoners who have had no food and very little protective clothing. Our Red Cross supplies would not be more than a drop in the ocean for these thousands and there was little we could do to help them. They peered in through the windows at us and hammered on the locked door and at the sight of these poor wretched people, our meal lost its savour.

After lunch we went back up the hill to our cookhouse and settled in. Russian planes appeared again in the afternoon and machine-gunned German lorries and troops in the field opposite us. The Medical Officers decided to move the sick in to the cellars and we spent a busy afternoon getting them fixed up. We have remained upstairs where we have lit fires to ward off the cold and damp.

We had another meal in the evening and as we were finishing the staff of Kopernikus moved in from their huts in the camp below. They feel that it is better for us all to be together. After dark a party took a wagon down to the

> Red Cross store and moved all our supplies up to our
> refuge. We had to make our way through hordes of Russian
> prisoners who are growing menacing with the relaxing
> of guarding by the Germans. We wish there was more we
> could do to help them but it is not possible.

In essence, there was a great deal more the British prisoners of war could
have done to help their Russian counterparts, but for whatever reason
they chose not to. They could have shared some of their food and clothes
with the by now desperate Russian prisoners, but they didn't. Read the
following paragraph of Leonard Parker's diary entry, and see how it
blatantly contradicts what he said in the previous one.

> The staff, most of whom are medical orderlies, have pooled
> all supplies and feed as well. Porridge in the morning with the
> inevitable tea, a good hot stew at dinner time, tea, Horlicks
> and Ovaltine galore. We who are fit are kept busy serving
> the bed patients who are all keeping cheerful despite their
> crowded condition in the cellars and the horrible suspense
> of just sitting here waiting for what?

By that time, the poorly clothed and extremely hungry Russians must
have been at their wits end, struggling to understand why, despite their
numbers, that their supposed allies in the same camp were not prepared
to help them with an offer of either food or clothes, no matter how small.
This was even more difficult to understand when the likelihood was that
in a very short period of time their location would likely be overrun
by elements of the attacking Red Army, whose officers would have no
doubt been none too pleased when they discovered the British prisoners
of war had failed to share their food and clothing supplies.

> Bob made a communal bed for the four of us, using all our
> blankets and greatcoats and we finally crawled in and slept
> soundly.

That was the end of the first day, and so far, so good. Although undoubtedly
extremely cold, the British prisoners of war had warm clothing, plenty of
food, no one had been hurt, wounded or killed. It was time to get a good

night's sleep and do it all over again the following day and hope they were still alive at the end of it.

Sunday 21 January 1945

Clear and cold this morning. The whole camp presented a strangely deserted air as I strolled out and had a look around. Although there are plenty of Russian prisoners to be seen wandering in and out of the compounds at will, there is not a single German to be seen. We wondered whether they had left us or whether we just could not see them in their defensive positions. In any case we are not being guarded. It is a strange sensation after being prisoners for so long, almost as if we were free, although I expect we would soon be stopped if we ventured outside the confines of the camp.

One of our Sergeant-Majors prepared a nominal roll of all of us this morning while another detailed a stick guard. So signs of regimental discipline are re-appearing after five years. But this place is full of thousands of desperate starving and dying Russian prisoners and we must be careful.

This afternoon, due to increased activity in the fields close by, we were all ordered to the cellars. It is very damp and cold down here and we miss the fires we had made upstairs. In addition we are horribly overcrowded, there being barely enough room to walk, and the French prisoners who have been moved up from the hospital add to the confusion by sprawling about, shouting and paying no attention to our officers in charge. But the staff continue to feed us well and we have cigarettes to smoke. Spirits high.

It is fairly quiet outside now with occasional bursts of machine gun fire. We have connected all cellars by hacking doorways from one to another so as to lessen the danger of any room being completely cut off in case of a fall of debris. It is bitterly cold now and the frost is thick everywhere. We have to cross a long open stretch to go to the latrines and it is under fire, but nature makes no concessions to war-fare. On the contrary, we find ourselves frequently 'engaged' and have to make the hazardous dash several times a day. While inside we can hear bullets pinging against the brickwork.

I understand from one of our own chaps who worked on this building that they didn't bother much about mixing strong concrete when they put it up. He said, exaggeratedly, I trust that a good rainstorm would wash away the cement from between the bricks. I investigated and found that I could easily pick it out with my fingers. What a shelter. I hope the wind doesn't get too strong or we may find ourselves buried before the Russians get here. Bob and Jack have made their bed near the door of the cellar over which hung a heavy blanket to absorb any blast. A door would be blown in on us. Mac and I are sleeping further inside the cellar but close at hand. We slept fairly well although we were a little cold.

Monday 22 January 1945

Today we contacted the first Russian forward patrols. At about 10 o'clock this morning two Russian soldiers appeared outside the wire and were spotted by one of our chaps. We had previously brought a Russian Colonel PoW into the cellars with us and he, speaking a little German which we could understand, acted as interpreter. It was impossible to understand a single word they said but they seemed friendly enough and grinned amiably at us. They ordered us to remain in the cellars at all times, told us that their main column would soon be here when we would be sent back down their lines. They wished us luck and disappeared, and we saw them no more today. Later in the afternoon, however, a Russian tank appeared, stopped on the road near us and a man dressed in a white sheepskin coat had a look round, but the tank soon made off again.

No Germans were to be seen and both these Russian scouting parties came and went unmolested. We thought this very strange but concluded that the Germans had fallen back to make a stand in Thorn.

The lack of activity by the Germans could have simply been down to self-preservation and a realisation that the war was finally lost. Opening fire on the advancing Russian soldiers would not have been a good thing to do, in fact it would have been totally futile. They at least had a chance to surrender, which was a much better option, especially for a group of men who no doubt knew that the war was a lost cause, and all they wanted to do was to survive, get back home to their families and get down to the job of rebuilding their lives.

Late this afternoon two troop dispersal shells burst directly over us, flinging whining pieces of shrapnel all about like a swarm of angry wasps. Many brave souls who had defied orders to remain below and were upstairs in the kitchen by the fire came rushing down the cellar steps like a stampede of wild horses. Several people were trampled underfoot in the rush and we nearly had some more patients. Bob, who had been standing in the doorway at the time of the explosions, was flung bodily back in to the cellar and crashed heavily in to a recumbent Frenchman. The Froggie set up a howl of protest and started abusing Big Jock in no uncertain terms. Bob picked himself up, relieved to find nothing broken, and gave the Frenchman one of his fiercest glares, whereupon he subsided into a low muttering and pursued the matter no further. The cookhouse chimney was destroyed and the kitchen filled with smoke and flying embers. Those who had been hugging the stove were black with soot and their clothes were smouldering. Everyone stayed in the cellars tonight; butterfly's [sic] were working overtime in my stomach.

At about 11 o'clock this evening the German Camp Commandant, a Hauptmann, appeared armed with a Tommy gun. He said that we were not to leave the camp and were to stay under cover at all times. When the Russians had been driven back, we would be transported to camps further inside Germany. He left soon after, blissfully unaware that all around him our chaps had been holding pick-staves, hatchets and crowbars behind their backs. If he had attempted to make us leave there and then, he would never have left the cellar alive.

It has been a beautifully clear day with very little signs of fighting. It is still cold and we must be careful of frostbite, so we took periodical little walks in the cellar to keep warm. An ominous stillness hung all over the camp. We learned from the German Hauptmann that a fierce battle had raged at the Training Ground a couple of miles away yesterday. Had we remained in Einheit Drei we would have been in the thick of it.

We are wondering how the main column is faring and what the outcome of yesterday's battle had been. It is getting very nerve wracking, just waiting like rabbits in a warren.

Tuesday 23 January 1945

Today is the day for which we have all waited for, talked of, dreamed of, for five long and dreary years. We are no longer prisoners of war. By inference it would seem that we are free! At least we are no longer held by the Germans. We are now in Russian hands. And yet none of us have the feeling of liberation. Perhaps it is a little too early for that.

An interesting point here is that there is no mention of the German guards under whose control they had previously been. Leonard's diary does not mention what happened to them. They might have simply run off before the Russians arrived so as not to be captured by them, fearing what would happen to them, taking into account previous wartime atrocities the Germans had carried out on Russian soldiers and citizens during Operation Barbarossa. They might have already surrendered to the Russians, hoping that by doing so they would be spared and taken as prisoners of war, or they might have tried to fight against overwhelming odds, and been killed in the process.

It is just strange that on Monday 22 January 1945, Parker talks about himself and his colleagues having been addressed by a German Hauptmann (Captain) and the next day they wake up in the hands of the Russians, but with no explanation as to how that came about.

Anyway, this morning the same two Russian forward scouts that had appeared yesterday came again to the wire and told us to leave the camp within ten minutes. After that they said they could not be responsible for our safety. Get out and move further down their lines, that was the order. And we didn't argue. They forbade us to take any kit whatsoever; there was no time. Chaos reigned! We grabbed whatever was nearest to hand, I managed to get my valise which was already packed, as did Bob, Mac and Jack and most of the others, but by far the greatest bulk of our kit was abandoned. Food, clothing, medical supplies, all were jettisoned. Even the emergency food packs which Jack had prepared so carefully against just such a contingency as this, were forgotten and left behind unopened. The main thing was to get to comparative safety with whole skins before things got too hot. And every other consideration was put out of mind in the mad scramble.

There were no gates in the wire at this part of the camp, and to go to the main entrance would have been to go towards the Germans. We had no wish to become the meat in the sandwich. What to do? Bob, Jack of all trades, had never failed us in the past and he rose to the present emergency magnificently. From nowhere he produced a large two handed axe and set to work on the wire with all his strength and Scots determination. One Russian POW was a bit too eager and nearly got decapitated for his pains. Bob was giving the axe all he had got and it was a good plan to give him plenty of room. Finally he made a gap big enough to pass through and we all streamed out on to the road. We hesitated there wondering whether to go back for some more kit; suddenly a bullet ricocheted close by with a single whine, and we hesitated no longer. Off we went as fast as we could go on the ice bound road. We passed several groups of Russian soldiers behind mobile machine guns but saw no heavy concentration of troops as yet. A farm horse and cart passed us, driven by a Mongolian-looking soldier; as it went past I glanced in and immediately wished I hadn't. It was loaded with stiffening bodies, all flung in helter-skelter, a sickening sight.

As we hurried on, Jack had an accident. He slipped on the ice and crashed heavily to the ground, twisting his Achilles tendon. Deciding that he was overloaded he set to work there and then, in the middle of the road and amidst a scene of confusion and rout, to sort out his valise and lighten his load. He urged us to push on which we did, and he caught us up later, hobbling along awkwardly and swearing that he would never fully recover the use of his ankle.

A little further on the whole party halted off the road to wait for stragglers and to reorganise. We formed ourselves into stretcher-carrying parties with a relief for each stretcher. After a brief rest we pushed on again. We were to make for a Russian headquarters where we were told we would be directed to billets and given food. The further we went the more Russians we saw, men, guns, lorries, horses, field kitchens, tanks, carts, all were mixed up together and streaming towards Thorn. At one point where we stopped to change over stretcher carriers, we talked in sign language, to a Russian soldier who seemed to have nothing else on his mind except to kill Germans.

The going was arduous over ice and our legs ached with the strain of trying to keep our balance and carrying stretchers.

At one brief halt I asked the chap on our stretcher, jokingly, how he would like me to drop something on his leg which was set in plaster. He turned green and groaned. Alarmed I asked Jack what was the matter. He laughed and said 'Bob just tripped over the bloke's leg.' I kept my mouth shut after that. Finally, when we felt we could not go on much further, we reached a tiny village. In one of the two or three houses there were, at long last, some Russians who seemed to know what to do about us. Here the stretcher cases and those too sick to walk were piled in to trucks and driven off. We were told to make for a village called Alexandrowo, where we could spend the night.

It was quite dark now and we pushed on against the packed stream of Russian convoys, unguided and unheeded by our 'liberators'. It was frightening to march on and on in the darkness, not knowing where we were going but following blindly the men in front and hoping the leaders knew the way. Besides, we were a small band to be in the midst of the attacking Russians, unable to speak to them or identify ourselves in the dark. At one point we had to feel our way along the edge of a terrifyingly high bank; there simply was no room on the road.

It was snowing now and we had to battle our way against a very keen wind and blinding snow. The going was getting harder and harder and, when the column left the road and made across the fields, our muscles cried out with the agony of lifting our legs knee-high at every step in the deep untrampled snow. My pack felt like a lump of lead and the shoulder straps cut like steel bands.

At long last and late at night, however, we found a firm road beneath our feet once more and were met by Poles with lanterns, who in some way or other, had been warned of our approach and were out searching for us. We had arrived at Alexandrowo.

Aleksandrów was a Polish town of three cultures and three religions. There were German Protestants, Jews who were in trade and, Catholic Poles. Until 1945, the richest and largest ethnic group were the Germans.

We were led into a large building and detailed off into rooms. What a relief to be indoors again. After the blinding snow and bitter cold and wet it seemed warm and snug inside and we threw ourselves thankfully on to the floor and rested. The place was full of Polish women and girls who brewed us some ersatz coffee and gave us bread to eat. It tasted like a home-cooked meal. We had eaten nothing all day. Jack, in some strange way managed to procure some more bread and a pot of jam so we ate our fill.

We smoked and stretched ourselves out, before we knew it we had dropped off into the sleep of utter exhaustion.

Wednesday 24 January 1945

I awoke feeling refreshed although very stiff this morning and after a breakfast of more substitute coffee and bread we were moved in to another room. This building had been a German Police school, a great rambling four-storied affair, and there was plenty of room. The place where we are now was the gymnasium, we have been able to dig out some iron cots and as Bob was able to get a coke fire built in the stove, we are at least warm. All our Red Cross food was left behind at the camp, however, and we are beginning to feel hungry. The only things we managed to salvage were some little bags of tea, sugar and milk; at least we are able to brew up.

The Polish girls are very kind and cannot do enough for us. It seems strange to be able to speak freely with women again.

After five years of being surrounded only by other men twenty-four hours a day, it must have been strange being so close to a female, let alone see one up close and being able talk to her. These men had been so used to other men's company there was a fair chance that many of them had forgotten how to conduct themselves in the presence of a woman. But this was just the beginning of their rehabilitation back into the life of being a civilian, that was assuming of course that they all actually survived the war and made it back home to the UK.

Mac and I made a tour of inspection of the whole building this morning. It is a vast place but is gradually filling up with refugees and Russian ex-prisoners of war. Everywhere we saw evidence of hasty departure by the Germans, papers strewn all over the floor, furniture pushed aside, neglected items of equipment and all manner of insignia, helmets, bits of uniform and rubbish thrown about in all the rooms. The Poles were busy cleaning up and had got a few Germans working. They were making these prisoners' lives a hell, forcing them to salute all Poles and Englishmen and driving them all day and all night. One, a young Police student of about 18, they played with as a cat plays with a mouse. Finally tiring of their sport, they shot him out of hand.

This evening we all went for a walk in the village and Bob put on his kilt in honour of the occasion of our first stroll as free men. He caused a minor sensation among the local inhabitants as they had never seen anything like it before.

A convoy of Russian armour had been engaging everyone's attention as they passed through, but when big Jock appeared on the scene, the spectators' interest switched to him leaving the charging Russians to go into battle unhonoured by the admiring cheers of the civilian population.

A friendly Pole took us visiting some of his friends and they regaled us with tales of the German occupation. He then took us to his home and gave us a glass of wine which nearly blew the top of my head off. They all take the line that they have merely changed the German taskmaster for a Russian one, and told us that the British must ally themselves with Poland to fight the Reds. And all of this before the war is even finished! Phooey to their ideas.

Thursday 25 January 1945

Tea in bed this morning. What a luxury, thanks to Mac who got up early and brewed up on the stove. We straightened up this morning and packed our kit in the hope we would be moving on today.

Bob has refused to see his way fit to sleep with Jack any more in future as he kicked Bob out of bed twice during the night and Big Jock had to finish his sleep as best he could on a foot-wide wooden form.

After a lunch of barley stew and bread, a Russian officer appeared and ordered us to move off to a place called Ciechocinek or Hermansbadd in German. It was bright out but cold and we were glad to keep moving. It was about a seven mile march and we arrived there as evening was closing in.

After the German invasion of Poland on 1 September 1939, which in essence was the beginning of the Second World War, Ciechocinek became incorporated into the Reichsgau Wartheland, on 26 September 1939, becoming part of the district of Hermannsbad, and remained so until the end of the war. If that wasn't bad enough, Poland was also invaded by Russia on 17 September 1939, the two invading countries splitting Poland between them. During the war the town included a German military hospital, and was also a health resort for German citizens. The town is situated about twenty kilometres south-east of Torun.

There was some confusion as to where we were to be billeted but this was finally sorted out and we moved in to what had been a private hotel and latterly used by the Germans as a hospital. Some of the party were accommodated in the main building, a large house, while the rest of us went in to the annexe. Bob, Mac, Jack and I took over a small room with two beds, a wardrobe, washstand and tiled stove. It is quite comfortable and at least good shelter.

No sooner had our people moved in than they were all over the place on foraging parties. The Germans had left behind quite a bit of their supplies and, among other things, we 'won' a few potatoes, half a dozen onions, a couple of custard powders, a little preserved fruit and some coal. We soon had a fire going in the stove and made a meal of sorts. A Polish girl came round and gave us some milk. From her we learned that the Germans had penetrated into the Russian lines and were even then only half a mile away on the other side of the river. Not a very comforting thought.

We all had a good wash down with water heated on the fire and I rinsed my underclothes in the soapy water. Felt better for this and we finally turned in at half-past twelve. Bob and Mac occupied one bed, Jack and I the other.

Friday 26 January 1945

I must say that I think Bob had grounds for his refusal to share Jack's bed. I passed a restless night.

We had a drink of tea this morning as it is holding out quite well, although the sugar and milk is all gone. After washing and shaving we all repacked our kit and sat down to wait further orders. None came. There is no news whatsoever regarding a further move.

We were all called out on parade this afternoon and were formed in to platoons. Bob, Mac and I were taken into

No.1 Platoon under Jack as Platoon Sergeant. The entire
body has been formed into a species of military formation
with Major Fulton, the dentist, as Commanding Officer,
Captain Feltham, the Medical Officer, as Adjutant, two
Company Sergeant Majors, four platoon Sergeants and
appropriate section leaders.

The Allied Prisoners of War List for the Second World War showed a
Captain 42671 R.J. Feltham, but nothing else about him.

It has started to snow again and we are glad to sit by our
stoves. At least we are warm. At dinner time we were given
a ladle of an indeterminate stew and a bread ration. By the
time we went to bed the snow had piled up thickly and it is
growing colder.

Saturday 27 January 1945

Roll call at half-past nine this morning. This is now a daily
occurrence. There was nothing to do afterwards but go back
to our room, have some dry toast and a drink of unsweetened,
un-milked tea, and sit and talk.

This afternoon Mac and I went out on a party to fetch
blankets. The snow was still falling, lying deep on the
ground and accompanied by a bitter frost in the morning.
We had to walk quite a distance for the blankets, loaded
them on to a little handcart and brought then back to the
billets for distribution.

We still had a little stock of coal and our room is warm
and cosy. At teatime we made up a stew from the supplies
we had foraged, with a watery custard and preserved fruit to
follow. Afterwards we sit around the stove and talk of home.

Jack's Achilles tendon has now become a source of
great amusement to all of us, although he maintains that
it is no laughing matter. I have an unforgettable memory
of his hobbling slowly down the room on the first day at
Alexandrowo. He was limping heavily and was bent

nearly double with stiffness from carrying his pack on the nightmare march the day before. Every picture tells a story, so they say, and to intents and purposes he looked about ninety years old with one foot in the grave and the other on a slippery pavement. We felt sorry for him but could not help laughing. He received our jibes with an air of quiet dignity. When we asked him what he had in his valise that weighed so heavily he produced hundreds of photographs, theatre programmes, posters and innumerable souvenirs. Big Jock glared at him.

'I suppose,' he said sarcastically, 'that when we get hungry we can all have a nice snapshot sandwich.' But Jack didn't care. He is determined to get his precious mementos home safely. And I don't doubt that he will.

Mad Maxwell returned from a trip back to Alexandrowo and dropped in to tell us the news. The Russians have turned the Police School in to a hospital and it is packed with wounded. The Poles are apparently still running berserk with German prisoners. Last night they dragged a wounded officer out of the hospital by his hair, took him into the street and shot him. His body was still lying there when Maxwell left this evening.

Stragglers from the main party are turning up here in threes and fours with tales of hardship and exposure suffered on the march. Taffy James, an amiable little chap from the camp died during the first night. They had all been left in a field to manage the best they could. I am afraid that he will not be the only one, poor kid.

Sunday 28 January 1945

Our platoon was duty platoon today and Bob, Mac and I were on snow clearing until after 'breakfast'. Then back to our room to hug the fire and talk, there is nothing else to do. Consequently it was something of a relief to be put to work this afternoon clearing some rooms of stacked furniture in preparation for the arrival of more stragglers. The sick, who had been left at Alexandrowo to await transport were brought here today and a sick-bay had been fixed up against their coming. All the medical orderlies have been pressed into service to tend them. One, a mental patient, requires twenty-four hour attention to prevent him injuring himself.

Two Russian Majors made an appearance today and gave us the welcome information that we definitely are to be transported to Warsaw and thence home within the next two or three days. They have commenced to make a nominal roll of us for transmission to London. As none of the Russians have any knowledge of English, they are writing our names phonetically in Russian. I fail to see that the resulting list is going to be any use, particularly as they have not bothered to record our regimental numbers. However, we can only hope that some good does come of it since our folks at home can't have had any word from us since last November and, knowing the Red Army over-run Thorn, it must be like the awful suspense of 1940 all over again for them.

Our own doctor carried out a medical inspection today. Mercifully we have so far escaped lice, boils and the almost inevitable skin diseases resultant of under-nourishment and physical strain.

Today was something of a red-letter day for Jack. He attended his first civilian mass since 1940.

Monday 29 January 1945

Seventh day since our 'liberation'. It has stopped snowing but is still very cold. We spent a quiet morning in the room after roll call. Dinner time brought the all too familiar barley stew which blows us out for an hour or two but then leaves us as hungry as ever. We are feeling the lack of fats acutely, our skins are drying and the slightest cut takes days to close up and almost always festers.

The four of us went out for a short walk this afternoon to have a look around and to try to get a hair cut, but all the shops are empty and shut and the whole town is very still and deserted.

I tired quickly and made my way back to the billet leaving the others to follow later. Bob and Mac returned a couple of hours after Jack and produced, as the result of a mild foraging expedition, a couple of candles. These are a real god send as we have had to sit in darkness hitherto. We shall be able to have the added comfort of a light tonight.

The chaps in the room across from us pooled their meagre supplies with ours and we were able to mix up a kind of hot stew for supper. We decided to continue with this arrangement as long as our little stocks of vegetables hold out.

I have decided to record herein the more important rumours which fly around with bewildering rapidity. Where they come from no one knows but come they do, thick and fast. Today's crop: The whole of Stalag XXA has been released: the Allies have 'landed' in Hamburg, Berlin and Gydnia. How they have landed and what they are doing now that they have done so, was not specified.

The snow started to come down in soft, thick, flurries again this evening and a biting wind is whistling around our window. Slept fitfully all night and had a most vivid dream of returning home. Jack has grown disgusted with our moaning at his restlessness in bed and has decided to sleep on the floor by himself.

We are not too badly off here; the food is not sufficient but fairly regular, we have warmth and good shelter from the weather. But the constant strain of waiting and hearing no news is beginning to take its toll on our nerves. At any rate we are well rid of the Frenchmen who were a constant source of annoyance to us at the cellars of Kopernikus. Crowded as we were there, they insisted on walking around incessantly, chattering and singing at the top of their voices. They got on our nerves in no small degree and Smithy got in to the habit of trampling on them ruthlessly whenever he moved about, at which their tongue wagging would change to pitiful, pleading cries of 'M'sieu, M'sieu', to which Big Jock paid no attention at all but continued his merciless footwork.

If only we could get a definite line on when we might reasonably expect to move on, it might make waiting a little more tolerable. But it is this constant state of anxiety and ignorance of our destiny that is making us despondent.

It was interesting to read Parker's description of his frustration at not knowing what was going on, or when they would begin their journey home. He had been in captivity for nearly five years before he left camp XXA, and human nature being what it is, uncertainty breeds concern, which leads to worry, anxiety, and even paranoia.

Between January and April 1945, an estimated 80,000 British and Allied prisoners of war, were force-marched across Poland, Czechoslovakia and Germany, in an effort to move them as far away as possible from the advancing Russian armies in the east, in what can only be described as severe weather conditions. This caused many of them severe hardship, starvation, injuries and in some cases, even death.

Tuesday 30 January 1945

It was a little bit warmer this morning but still quite cold with occasional snow. I heated a basin full of water on the stove, a saucepan at a time, before changing completely and washing out all of my underclothing, shirt and socks.

Dinner today consisted of stew, unsweetened custard which tasted like billposters paste, gooseberries and tea without milk. This afternoon we heard that a barber's shop in the town was going to open so we went down to try our luck. Unfortunately, after we had waited for an hour or more the barber still hadn't turned up. We shall soon have to cut each other's hair I think.

More arrivals from the main party including Johnny Gaskin, Wally Kersey, and Jimmy Woolcock who had a hair raising tail, embellished of course, in the Woodcock style. They have all been accommodated here and we understand that this town is to be made a collecting centre for released prisoners of war.

I checked the British Prisoners of War list for the period of the Second World War, and found a Gunner 1508965 Johnny W. Gaskin, who served with the Royal Artillery and had been a prisoner of war at Stalag 344 camp, which was located at Lambinowice, as well as a Lance Bombardier 1492585 Jimmy S. Woolcock, who also served with the Royal Artillery, and had been a prisoner of war at Stalag XXA, in Torun. I also found Rifleman 68989753 W.L. Kersey of the Kings Royal Rifle Corps, who had been a prisoner of war, but I could not find the camp at which he was held.

> Signs are being erected on all roads nearby directing stragglers to us. This is quite a good omen, for the larger our party grows the more insistent we can be to be afforded transportation homewards. The men are becoming extremely impatient as is only natural, and we are certainly not being given the treatment we have a right to expect as allies. There are, however, no signs at all of any road or rail facilities coming our way yet.
>
> Our personal supplies are now very low and we had a supper of sorts of boiled potatoes and gooseberries.

Wednesday 31 January 1945

Rumour this morning that rail connection has now been established between Alexandrowo and Warsaw and hopes run high in consequence of an early move in that direction and of being flown from there to England. In addition the Russians have asked for lists of names and addresses of next of kin to be prepared.

Bob, Mac and I were on fatigues this morning shifting more furniture until dinner time. I did not feel the need of so much stew to fill me up and the others said the same. This is not a good sign as it means that our systems are weakening and nature is trying to adjust herself to our shortened rations. I can't keep the barley down and have already had one or two attacks of vomiting accompanied by severe stomach pains.

Bob, Mac and Jack went out for a breath of fresh air after dinner but I stopped in and did some washing. At least we have a little soap and manage to keep ourselves reasonably clean. Tea was a weird mixture of boiled onion, dry toast with a little Bovril and sugarless tea.

George Twocock, a genial Canadian who was our Christmas guest in the room party at Konheit Drei, dropped in to our room for a chat this evening and we managed to pass a pleasant couple of hours.

I believe the man referred to could be Corporal SB 97229 George Twocock of the Royal Canadian Engineers.

In the midst of our talk, Maxwell returned from one of his jaunts to Alexandrowo and presented us with a small piece of fat, a few saccharine and a candle from one of our Polish friends. Thank goodness for the candle as we have been sitting in the dark again these last few nights.

Many chaps are talking of leaving here and trying to make their own way to Warsaw, Lublin or Odessa. I think this is a very risky business because, although we do not get much to eat here, at least we get something which is more than one might get on the road; there is safety in numbers here, whereas it would be very dangerous to wander about in small unidentified bands among these suspicious Russians; and above all, we have no maps nor any idea in which direction these places lie.

Chapter Five

The Diary of Leonard J. Parker –
Part Two: February 1945

Tuesday 1 February 1945

It is clear that the sense of euphoria initially felt by Leaonard Parker and his fellow prisoners of war when they discovered their German guards had abandoned them and set them free has long since dissipated. They have started to become enveloped by an overwhelming mixture of anxiety, stress, and strain at the situation in which they find themselves, and it is starting to take its toll on each and every one of them.

Thaw set in today and wet feet are commonplace. The weather is warmer but still windy and unpleasant. No change in the deadly routine of roll call, dinner, supper, and bed. We are all feeling the strain of inactivity and are going nearly mad with the desire to be on our way. Tempers are short and arguments are quick to flare up. Even the four of us, who are very close friends at heart, are beginning to get on each other's nerves a little.

One or two more arrivals today and we heard that the Russian authorities are rounding up all spare files and sending them in here to Ciechocinek.

I am sleeping badly now. We invariably go to bed hungry and with nothing to occupy our minds except thoughts of repatriation which is now so near and yet so very far away. One could reconcile oneself in the prison camp for we knew we would have to wait until the war was over, but now that we are in allied hands, we feel that we cannot endure much more of this uncertainty and that the Russians should have shipped us out long since. As soon as I shut my eyes at night I find myself walking up to the front door at home and greeting my folks. I am beginning to dread the long nights filled with sleeplessness and fitful dreams of being home.

Today's rumour for what it is worth: We move on Monday the 5th.

Friday 2 February 1945

Ground soaking wet and pools of water everywhere. We were duty platoon today but beyond routine tasks of yard cleaning, we were not called on for any fatigues. Bathing parades were inaugurated as the Russians have got a neighbouring bath house, however Bob and I had another wash down in our room before turning in.

At four o'clock this afternoon we all paraded to be addressed by Captain Lake who is now the adjutant; Captain Feltham finds his time too fully occupied in tending the sick. He told us that our names and numbers have been forwarded to Moscow for onward transmission through the British authorities to London, so our people should soon know we are safe. Also the Russians have promised that we shall be moved as soon as transport is available, when we shall receive priority. All this was very heartening and we feel that when the great day does come it will be well worth waiting for.

The Russians have now, for some reason best known to themselves, forbidden us to take walks around the town and neighbouring villages during certain hours and after dark. An English picquet has been posted to enforce this and Mac was on the first spell. Great indignation is felt on this curb to our only recreation, the Russians are treating us more and more as if we were their prisoners and not allies. Mac, in addition to his picquet duty this morning was medical attendant to the mental patient all night.

Saturday 3 February 1945

Big Jock and I are now on permanent yard cleaning duty which precludes us from being called on for other fatigues. Half an hour after roll call sees the job done and we are free of duties for the rest of the day, unless our platoon is on potato peeling, in which case we have to turn out with the others.

A very mild day with a warm sun shining like spring. I felt too tired to go outside however, and slept this afternoon until four o'clock when we rewarmed a little stew left over from dinner. We can hardly look a plate of this mess in the face without feeling sick, but it's all we have: 'ya gotta eat'.

Maxwell came in this evening and we spent the time talking. I slept a little better tonight, although my stomach is upset and full of wind. Our rations have practically run out now, we are on our last tin of Bovril which we spread on dry toast. The Russians give us nothing to spread on dry toast. The Russians give us nothing to spread on the bread ration. In fact, all we get from them is the nauseous barley stew at dinner time and a hunk of bread at night; no margarine, no fat of any kind, very little meat in the stew together with barley and potatos; and that's all. It would be more understandable if they had not got the stuff to give us, but as we know that they are well supplied with American tinned food and fresh meat which they slaughter themselves. The only 'rations' they give us are from captured stocks of German food.

Sunday 4 February 1945

Awoke this morning with severe stomach pains and an attack of chronic diarhea [*sic*]. Feeling very sick indeed. I spent the morning lying on the bed, had no breakfast and two pieces of rough dry toast and a drink of weak tea for dinner.

There were strong rumours of a move by train tomorrow. It would be just my luck for it to come after all this time now that I am under the weather. So strong were the rumours that

Bob and Mac packed their kit in readiness this afternoon. But Jack could not work up any belief in the rumour and refused to pack anything. Felt too rotten to get up at all and stayed in bed.

Both Bob and Mac went out this afternoon, Jack was busy elsewhere, and I stayed in bed. Bowels strained and stomach very painful; attacks of vomiting leaves me weak. I had a couple of slices of dry toast and a drink of weak tea about six o'clock. Feeling very grubby and sticky I managed to get up to wash and shave this evening, but had to prop myself up on the washbasin with one hand; I felt better and a little refreshed but very weak and faint when I stand up. The others came in after I had crawled back to bed and were very sympathetic, but there was little they could do to help. Mac advised me not to eat anything at all until the diarrhea [*sic*] had passed, and consequently I feel very hungry.

Fortunately there are two lavatories in this building and I am kept busy dragging myself from bed to one or the other!

There has been no official news of a move, but hopes are high for tomorrow. This is really the strongest rumour we have had to date, though we can't pin down any authoritative origin and many are frankly doubtful. We have been disappointed in this way before. The rumour has it that hospital care will be available for the sick, and the way I feel at the moment, I shall need one of them. I sincerely hope that I feel better tomorrow and that we shall go on our way. I think that would be as good as a tonic, to know that we were moving towards England and home again, I can stand feeling sick.

Monday 5 February 1945

Stomach pains still present this morning but not quite so severe as yesterday. Nor is the diarrhea [*sic*] so troublesome although it has not yet gone and I am still feeling weak. Accordingly I kept on dry toast and only a very little soup at dinner time. I do not feel anywhere near normal yet, but I dare to hope that I have got over the worst of the attack.

This morning I had a very good wash, tidied up my kit and washed my clothing just in case anything should come of the rumoured move. Anyway, I felt better for a clean change and for having things neat and tidy once more. We were doomed to disappointment again, however. There are no further signs of a shift from here despite the strong talk of it yesterday. This is hard to hear, for no matter how sceptical we are of these rumours, we cannot help but feel a little ray of hope when we hear them and there is always a keen sense of frustration when they come to naught.

We are now completely out of 'spread' for our bread, and having to eat it dry. It is awful tasting muck without something to help it down, is practically unpalatable. Mac put his inventive genius to work and produced a spread made of a mixture of some rhubarb, pudding powder and saccharine. It certainly has a very distinctive taste, but it really does help and we passed a vote of thanks to Mac. I fear however, he would not make his fortune if he tried to market his product.

The others went out this afternoon to see what they could find and returned with dental wax for melting down into night lights, and a little bacon fat. Thereupon we made a meal of bread and fat, and tea without sugar.

After we had finished eating, George Twocock and Maxwell came in to spend the evening talking. As always the conversation turned to arriving home, what we would do and when we thought it might come about. Just for the fun of it we decided to try to forecast the date when we would get back and for purposes of checking I recorded them herein. Here they are:-

Jack: He said we will be home and well settled by 28th Feburay 1945.

Bob: Was rather undecided but finally prophesised that he would be home by his next birthday, 9th March 1945.

Max: Said he expected to dock at a British port by 10th March 1945.

Mac: Thought he might not be actually in his own
         home, but expected to be in England at least by
         14th March 1945

George: Having three thousand miles or more further to
         travel than any of us, refused to commit himself.

Len: I am afraid I felt in rather a pessimistic mood this
         evening and would not venture a guess.

Tuesday 6 February 1945

Alarums and excursions! The whole place was fairly
humming this morning with talk of a move at ten o'clock.
This did not materialise but was whittled down to the fact
that we are now under one hour's notice and as soon as the
train arrives we shall be off. This is very encouraging, but
personally I do not need an hour's notice. I'll be out of here
in five minutes if they ever say the word. We even went so
far as to roll up our blankets and lash them onto our packs in
readiness but the day went by and nothing happened, except
that Mac got stuck on picquet duty.

Twenty or so American officers turned up here late this
afternoon under a Colonel and they said that there were more
on their way. Except for one or two American soldiers who
passed through Einheit Drei, these are the first of their kind
we have seen and we are quite impressed. They are fine big
chaps with a swaggering devil may care attitude and all vow
they will not remain here very long. They were surprised
to learn that we have been here for nearly two weeks. Their
Colonel, too, is a very live wire and we hear that he has not
yet actually arrived but has stayed behind in Alexandrowo
to meet some high ranking Russians and demand that he
and his men be given facilities for proceeding on their
way. Perhaps we may get some action now. Jack knowing
my interest in Americans enquired if there were any Baltimoreans among them, but they were mostly southerners.

We had a tea of dry toast and weak tea and then turned in. I find that I am taking a very long time to get to sleep again and am all on edge and nervy.

Wednesday 7 February 1945

Our platoon was duty platoon today so Bob and I spent an hour after roll call cleaning up the yard. A little later Bob, Mac and I went out to an abandoned German dental surgery to collect furniture for a Russian woman dentist who was setting up shop in the large building where the Russians had set up an administrative centre. We found some dental wax which we shall be able to break up and use in our night lights.

The American Colonel arrived today and came up to expectations as a go ahead chap.

As if the food were not bad enough, it was almost un-eatable today owing to the fact that someone had put too much salt in it.

This afternoon Bob, Mac and I went down to the town to try to strike some sort of deal with a shopkeeper who had somehow managed to open his store. We managed to pry a little jam loose from him and I made my way back to billet leaving Bob and Mack to exploit a contact they had made with a couple of Polish civilians.

On the way back I met an Italian who had worked at Stalag. He told me that the plan was to send us home via Odessa, Black Sea, Greece, Egypt, etc. When I got back to the billet I borrowed a map of Europe and traced out this course. It certainly is a long trip but should prove an interesting one. Where the Italian got his information, I don't know, but he seemed quite sure of it.

Bob and Mac returned with riches, a jar of milk and some jam, which meant no more dry bread for a while, and a promise of more milk, meat and sugar.

In the midst of a targeted Russian offensive against the once great German Army, it was a minor miracle that there were that many buildings still standing, let alone any of them being a shop which could provide anything in the way of food stuffs.

I am feeling fitter now and a little more resigned to waiting, although the lack of discipline among some of our chaps causes some unpleasantness. This must be expected and endured, I fear. Tempers are very short and even between the four of us there is too much wrangling and argumentativeness. We must make a big effort to keep our tempers and tongues in check and be very, very patient.

The Russian civilians moved off from their HQ. Whether this heralds a move for us or not is a matter for conjecture.

Thursday 8 February 1945

This morning the American officers moved to new billets taking a British N.C.O. and five men with them. They will live better than us as the Americans manage, in some mysterious fashion, to procure better rations than ours. Consequently they are greatly envied.

Bob and Mac were out 'flapping their wings' again today following up their contact of yesterday. Jack went out too after dinner and I stayed in and had a bath and prepared a meal of sorts against their return. They were all very late in but Smithy and Mac brought some more milk and two lumps of salted meat in a glass jar. It looked a bit queer but we supposed it was a specimen of Polish cooking and decided to eat it anyway.

The weather has taken a turn for the better and although it is very damp underfoot, it is quite spring like with a bright sun and warm breeze. We are reasonably comfortable here but the food question is worrying and we are fed up to the teeth with barley and indigestible bread; but Bob and Mac's great effort will give us a change of diet for a couple of days. The most difficult part of our enforced stay here is the waiting. The constant strain of hoping and guessing and never having anything tangible to look forward to is almost intolerable and is taking a very noticeable toll of the men's health.

At a concert held in the Europa Café tonight, a Russian officer told the assembled released prisoners of war that things are going well for the Allies and that the Russian authorities hope to have us home soon, but their war effort must take precedence. Again nothing definite; his speech was greeted with ironic jeers and he retired in a huff.

Friday 9 February 1945

Mac and I went for a walk this morning to look for a barber's shop. We need haircuts badly! We found one but as we might have known, it was shut!

Some of the latest arrivals from Alexandrowo had told us that Winterbottom was on his way to join us, so Jack went off this morning to meet him on the road. He missed him however; we learned later that Winter had bypassed us and continued on his way to Warsaw with two Americans. This place is earning a bad reputation among stragglers as a dead end. Consequently most of them steer clear of us.

This afternoon Jack and I went back to the barber's shop which we found open, so we had our first haircut since two weeks before we left Keinnheit Drei. As Englishmen we were objects of some curiosity to the Poles there. They hesitated to speak to us as we knew no Polish and it is a risky business to speak German within earshot of the Russians. To them anyone who speaks German is German and gets treated accordingly. However, the Poles opened up eventually and we had a good chin wag. I felt sorry for then remaining in this benighted place and was glad to think that we shall get away, eventually!

Mac and Bob were not in this evening so Jack and I had a lonely tea and sat talking to George Twocock.

Today's news is good and bad. The bad part was information that a British plane on its way to a Moscow conference had crashed and all the passengers, including diplomats and a statesman, were killed.

There had been a Moscow Conference every year between 1941 and 1945, the one that took place between 9 and 19 October 1944, was the fourth. A main part of the conference was dedicated to how Eastern Europe was going to be divided between Russian and the Western powers, once the war was over and the Allied nations had become the victors.

The agreements that were struck at the conference gave the Russians the majority control of Poland, Romania, Hungary and Bulgaria, while the West would control the majority of Greece, and Yugoslavia would be split between Russia and the West.

Maybe the reason behind the continual delay in repatriating the British prisoners of war was also to do with the Moscow Conference. Stalin had agreed to come into the war on the side of the Allies against Japan, while Britain had agreed to return all Soviet citizens whom they had liberated from German captivity. Maybe Stalin was waiting to see if Winston Churchill would honour his part of the agreement before handing over British prisoners of war. Maybe they were being held as bargaining chips, just in case Churchill broke the promises he had made to Stalin at the Moscow Conference.

Russia did eventually declare war on Japan, but not for another ten months, on August 8 1945, just two days after the United States dropped their atomic bomb on Hiroshima and only six days before Japan announced its surrender. On 18 August 1945, Soviet forces landed on the Japanese islands of the Southern Kurils, also known as the Northern Territories.

> The news affecting us more intimately, however, was of a more cheering nature. It had an 'official' air to it, coming as it did in the 'Detail' for tomorrow which is given out through Platoon Commanders nightly. Jack, in his eternal quest for souvenirs , kept his copy:-
>
> **Details for Saturday 10 February 1945**
>
> Routine
> All ranks will parade at 0800 hours tomorrow, Saturday 10 February 1945 for an address by a Russian officer.
>
> Re: Evacuation of Released British Ps.O.W.
> In an interview today with the Russian Town Commandant the following information was given. The scheme for

evacuation by transport to a camp near Warsaw had been cancelled. Transport is now available but there is a possibility that another route will be taken.

The British Government has been informed of our presence in this district and has been asked by the Russian Government which route and means shall be used to return us to the United Kingdom. The reply of his Majesty's Government has not yet been received. When it is to hand, arrangements will be made to move us to the nearest port or assembly area where British ships or other transport can meet us. Meanwhile the only recognised collecting point is here.

Passes

All men going out must be in possession of a pass duly signed by a British officer.

Such passes will be issued freely. Before proceeding out the pass must be collected at the Orderly Room and returned again, immediately on arrival back.

Signed S. Darley, CSM

9th February 1945.

This news of evacuation has perked us up a bit and everyone is decidedly more cheerful. Squabbling and tempers are not so quick to flare up when news is good. But the business of passes, 'Orderly Room' and attempts at regimentation in our present circumstances is rather stupid and bitterly resented by most. Today even more men 'deserted' the camp and pushed on, on their own.

Saturday 10 February 1945

Paraded at 9 o'clock this morning to hear the address by a Russian Colonel who is in charge of released personnel. He spoke no English, of course, but his speech was translated to us. He corroborated yesterday's official statement and warned us once more against making our own way. It will be much quicker, he said, to wait for the mass move which will not be long in starting. This sounds good but, having been disappointed too often in the past, we are sceptical. We are waiting now for the advice from the British Government as to our disposal.

I changed my underclothes, shirt and socks this morning and did all my washing. I like to have my things clean in case of a sudden move, although the soap is ill-afforded. We managed to bring a little with us but it is running very short now. We have been generously given an issue by the Russians, one bar of RIF between three. Shades of 1940!

Spent a quiet afternoon with no further signs of moving. Rumour spread around that we must all be moved out of these buildings by Wednesday as they are turning this place in to a hospital base. I fear, however, that will not herald a move homewards but merely to other billets where we would have to go all through the dreary business of settling in again and face another interminable period of waiting. The monotony here is deadly. Same routine day in and day out, even week in, week out. It would be such a wonderful feeling if we were moving , even slowly, on our way. But we get no further.

Sunday 11 February 1945

A novel experience this morning. It was our platoon's turn for baths and we duly paraded and marched over to the bath house across the road. It was quite a good place with plenty of room for our clothes and ample showers. We were about half undressed when the door opened and a Russian woman attendant walked through and passed in to the shower rom. There were howls of protest from all the chaps which went completely unnoticed. These people think nothing of it. We stood undecided for a moment, but we had to have baths. As we showered dried ourselves and dressed again several women attendants came and went, paying not the slightest attention to our outraged modesty. Never again thanks!

Barley soup with half cooked carrots for dinner. What wouldn't we do to a Red Cross parcel now.

There was a dance at the Europa Café this evening which was liberally attended by our chaps. Russian women soldiers were there in plenty and a good time seemed to be had by all. It went on till about four o'clock in the morning, but was marred, I fear, by drunken Red Army soldiers who are very belligerent and even dangerous in their cups.

We are still hanging on waiting further instructions regarding a move. Each day brings us a little nearer, I suppose, but it is really maddening just sitting around with nothing to do, nothing to read, just waiting, waiting. And we can't do anything to help speed things up. Just wait, We get promises galore, rumours are as thick as flies round a jampot, and our hopes build up and then get dashed to earth again, time after time. Its enough to drive us to drink, if we had anything to drink.

Monday 12 February 1945

Monday, and the start of yet another week in this wretched dump. The spring like weather which made us all feel a little more lively has gone again, and it has started to snow again this morning, thick and fast. The ground was soon covered and winter is once more with us cold and wet.

We heard today that the American Colonel, who has been paying daily visits to the Russian Commandant to demand transport, has been promised it within the next five days and in addition the Belgians have been told to stand by for a thirty-six hours' train journey.

But today's biggest buzz, one which caused one of those minor sensations which sweep through the camp periodically, was that a plane has left Moscow, been to London and returned with a committee who have dealt with the question of the disposal of released British prisoners of war. So once again our hopes are raised and we are expecting something definite with regard repatriation this week. All this coupled with the Russian promise, for what it is worth, to the Americans, the warning to the Belgians and the general expectations of a move on within the next five days.

For tea we had jellied meat, bread and butter and ersatz coffee tonight.

We are all fit as we can expect to be on these rations and are duly thankful. But there can be no doubt that this constant state of anxiety and nervous tension is weakening to our physical as well as our mental conditions.

Tuesday 13 February 1945

Jack out 'sightseeing' this morning, although what he can find of interest in this benighted blot on the map is beyond me.

Mac and Bob took turns today in working in the Russian Dental Centre where Captain Cook, our own Dental Officer, is lending a hand. His interest, we think, is not so much the ever increasing line of patients, but rather the dentist who is, surprisingly, a woman. These Russians seem to use women in all manner of jobs which they seem to do as ably as men with no regard to differentiation between the sexes. Witness the bath house episode.

No news, which, if we are to believe the old saying, is good news. This afternoon I got hold of a book, praise Allah! At last something to read, something to take my mind off our worries here. I lay down in the room this afternoon, all the others were out, and had a good book soak. It is only a very ordinary 'who dunnit' but if it were the greatest masterpiece ever put on paper, I could not enjoy it more. It is a real treat, the best thing I have had since we left Einheit Drei. Where it came from originally, I don't know, but I wouldn't give it up for all the tea in China until I have read every last page, including the advertisements on the covers.

When the other chaps came in we had a supper of sorts, argued for an hour or so, and turned in.

I am afraid this waiting business is playing Old Harry with our tempers and we are all getting on each other's nerves. The slightest remark is enough to send us all off in to heated wrangling when we all say things that we don't really mean. Tempers flare up like sulphur matches at the least provocation. This sitting around is one of the hardest things we have had to endure yet.

Wednesday 14 February 1945

This morning we were all paraded to hear yet another address by yet another Russian Colonel. We formed into a hollow square, there was the usual business of being called to attention, exchange of salutes between our officers and the Russians, and then he strode into the middle and glared around at all of us. We waited expectantly. Suddenly he drew himself up, took a deep breath and then, at the top of his voice, bellowed, 'GOOD DAY'. We looked at each other with uncertainty. Was he finished before he had even began? But that was only the beginning. He then launched in to vitriolic harangue, working himself up into a near frenzy as he warmed to his task. And it was all in Russian. We didn't understand a word he said beyond his initial greeting, upon which, no doubt, he prided himself as a linguist. When he had finished however, the whole thing was translated to us. With all the trimmings cut out, it boiled down to a bitter attack on the fact that many of our chaps had seen fit to go on their way without further recourse to the Russian in charge. This he said was bad in many ways. He painted lurid pictures to us of our men laying out in the wastes, frozen or starving to death, beset by wolves, bands of Germans or murderous Poles. His Government, he went on, considered this a serious affront to their hospitality. Had they not done everything for our comfort? Had they not gone out of their way to treat us as honoured friends and allies? Had they not …. His list of the wonderful things they had done for us, was unending. Of course all of his questions could be answered in one word, 'No'!! And he left out, to my way of thinking, the greatest danger of all, that of his fellow soldiers, who, drunk or sober, would not weigh too heavily the consequences of robbing isolated men.

He informed us in conclusion that here we were and here we would stay until a competent British authority arrived to conduct us to an assembly point. He walked off parade to the accompaniment of an angry murmuring and one or two impolite noises from the rear ranks. But for all our defiance we were plunged in to gloom. Does this mean an even longer period of just sitting round in helpless, maddening inactivity?

But rumour reared its head again this afternoon and said that a Russian officer has arrived here to take us to a new camp. We don't know what to think. I read and slept this afternoon and then we had our frugal supper and went to bed as usual. The five days are running out and we are still here.

Although this was understandably a frustrating time for Leonard and his fellow prisoners of war, there was a bigger picture which, although it included them, didn't necessarily place them at the front of the queue when it came to the Allies' list of priorities.

Just four months after the fourth Moscow Conference in October 1944 came the Yalta Conference, which took place between 4 and 11 February 1945 in the Crimea. This saw the leaders of the 'Big Three' of America, Britain and Russia, sit down to discuss the shape of post-war Europe. It was decided that Germany would be split in to four zones, that would each be administered by one of the following countries, America, Britain, France and Russia

On the evening of 13/14 February 1945, the RAF carried out a massive air raid on the German city of Dresden. The bombardment, which was carried out by 805 aircraft of the RAF's Bomber Command, triggered one of the worst firestorms of the Second World War. It has been estimated that at least 55,000 people, nearly all of whom were civilians, perished as a result of the bombings.

With the war still going on, and the British heavily involved in the Allied push on the Western Front, operational needs were always going to supersede less important ones, such as collecting a number of stranded prisoners of war. Putting it bluntly, why would the British authorities utilise much-needed equipment and manpower, and divert them to Poland to collect these men, many of whom had been prisoners of war for some five years.

However frustrating the circumstances that Leonard and his comrades found themselves in, this was the reality of their situation.

Thursday 15 February 1945

Signs of activity this morning. Without any warning we were confined to our billets to await a final registration and the issue of some sort of identity cards, and the rumour was that a train was coming for us from thirty-five kilometres away. When the registration was completed and the train had arrived we would be on our way.

I did a complete wash this morning. The snow had started to fall again and is thick everywhere.

Our turn for registration did not come until this evening and I went over to face an hour's queueing. While waiting I talked with Alan Massingham who had just returned from a trip to Thorn. He said that all the Englishmen there had been collected and registered. His other news was that Thorn is not too badly knocked about, but that Stalag XXA is stripped of everything worth having, Red Cross books, clothing, medical supplies, all had been looted. Kinheit Drei, he said had been burned to the ground in the fierce battle that had raged there.

After registration I went back to our room for tea, followed soon after by 'supper' of custard with milk, bread and butter and German coffee unsweetened, and then it was time for bed.

Friday 16 February 1945

Snowfall stopped and sun shining, but there was a cold wind blowing. Feeling the need for exercise, Jack and I went for a long walk this morning and saw an old church, some Abbey ruins and a Polish village. Apparently when the Germans had been retreating, they forced all the villagers in to the church and ignited fuses to gunpowder dumps in the crypt before pulling out. The Poles, however, at the last moment, managed to break down the locked doors and extinguish the fuses, this saving the lives of the whole village as well as their old church.

We met an old Pole who spoke a queer mixture of English and American slang. He said he had lived in Chicago, Goddam!

Still the same routine and no news. We are constantly hearing rumour upon rumour, trains expected, a complete shifting of all released prisoners by such and such a route and such and such a date, transport by lorries, etc., but none of these materialise. The latest is that the Russians are laying a third rail on the Polish lines, the gauge varies for Russian and German rolling stock. The Germans had re-laid the lines in all their captured territory. This conversion for the Russian trains is said to be complete from Warsaw to Posen, and when laid from Posen to Gnydia we shall be on our way. We are completely talked out of all possibilities and are still just, waiting!

Saturday 17 February 1945

Jack has been pressing, through our officers, for the last week or so for a truck to go to Thorn to see what could be salvaged from the wreck of Stalag XXA for our comfort. Finally the Russians agreed and he went off this morning with a party to see what they could find.

We were duty platoon this morning with Mac i/c in Jack's absence. This meant spud-peeling and poor Mac spent the whole morning keeping the chaps from slipping away. Some of us were on fatigues chopping wood for the bath house. We were interested to examine an Army truck of American make. It was quite unlike anything we had ever seen before, very powerful, front and back wheel transmission and well suited for its job. The Russian driver, when he saw us looking at a splintered hole in the windscreen, told us a great tale by means of signs and a few words of German and Russian, of how he had fought hand to hand with a party of German soldiers who had ambushed his truck, and how he had killed them all.

Spent a quiet afternoon by myself until Jack returned. His party brought books in plenty, and a few medical supplies. Jack had been on a little fragging expedition of his own in his old haunts, the Parcels Office. There he found, exactly where he had hidden it weeks before, a little cache of a large tin of Ovaltine, a tin of cheese and a tin of Marmite. It seems incredible that these should have survived the relentless pillaging that had gone on at Stalag XXA, but they were there. We decided to make these our 'iron rations' for the move, if ever a move does come.

Jack was very tired after his long day and we turned in early. I hear that Padre Latham is to set up a library with the books they have brought from Thorn. This is indeed wonderful news and I look forward to having plenty to read.

Sunday 18 February 1945

Jack's Polish friend from Alexandrowo turned up this morning while he was at Church. He went away when I told him where Jack was, but he returned later with Jack and made us a most welcome present of half a dozen candles. We have been sitting in darkness every night, or at best a gloom lit by the fitful light of two small nightlights fed with dental wax, so these candles are truly a magnificent gift.

No news with regard to moving. It looks as if we are destined to stop here for a hell of a long time yet. How long we shall be able to stand the monotony and the ever decreasing rations is problematical. The only bright spot at the moment is that the books will be available tomorrow.

Late tonight some Polish troops passed through the town. They were to spend the night here on their way up to the front. Jack got hold of two of them, both officers, but one a man and the other a woman of about twenty-two, and brought them up to our room for a talk. They told us that they had been in the underground movement but had joined the regular forces when the Russians came through. I was interested to hear that although there were whole battalions of Poles, they were almost entirely commanded by Russian officers. They were both fine looking people and very casual about their exploits. The girl was particularly attractive and it seemed horribly strange to us that she should live and fight at the front as a man. But she seemed to find nothing odd in it. Like the Russians they make no differentiation at all between the sexes. We wished them the very best of luck, pressed a few cigarettes on them and watched them go off to re-join their unit, then we took to our beds.

Monday 19 February 1945

'Latham's Library' opened this morning and I was on hand to get a couple of books. There was quite a good selection and I settled down to a day of good reading. This made the time pass quickly.

Spent a quiet uneventful day reading, had dinner and read again until tea time. Then suddenly, I was overcome by a terrible feeling of faintness and nausea. I could not stand on my feet without feeling as if I were going to keel over, so I lay down on the bed and rested until about eight o'clock. Then I had a cup of coffee (ersatz) and a couple of pieces of dry bread with the others and went to bed. Even when I lay down I felt waves of sickness pass all over me and the room seemed to be spinning around and the bed to be bumping up and down. Slept very fitfully and was glad when morning came.

These spells of sickness weaken me terribly and are very frightening. I know that the lack of exercise does me no good and Jack, Mac and Bob are forever urging me to go walking with them, but I'm worried for fear I might go out and be taken really bad. All three of them do everything they can but without medical supplies there is not much help they can give. I expect it is merely an accumulation of insufficient food, mental anxiety and being generally run down.

Tuesday 20 February 1945

George Twocock and Jack went off this morning to Alexandrowo intending to spend the night there with some Polish friends of theirs. I was surprised, therefore, when they returned about four o'clock this afternoon. They were both obsessed with the idea of pulling out and pushing on towards Warsaw with two American officers whom they had met on the road and who were waiting just outside Ciechocinek while they picked up their kit. I tried to dissuade Jack from going because I felt it to be highly dangerous, but he was determined. I felt too sick to go with him even had I been so inclined and I was dismayed at the thought of him going. Bob and Mac were not in at the time to lend support; indeed they might have gone with him. He went over to see Captain Lake, however, and after a stormy scene during which Lake forbade him to go, he came back to the room and told George that he was staying for the time being. I was relieved. Besides all other considerations I would have missed him. George decided that he was going anyway and we said goodbye to him rather reluctantly. He was a good chap and we liked him immediately. We were sorry to lose our 'Canuck'.

Knowing Jack to be feeling rather out of sorts at having his plans changed, I felt it better to keep off the subject. I am feeling a little better today but have been taking it very easy, just lying down and reading. The food is getting worse, if that is possible. There was just plain barley and boiled potato's [sic] for dinner today and dry bread at teatime. The food situation is precarious and unless we get a move on soon we shall be faring very poorly indeed. And yet rumours tell us that the situation is even worse in Warsaw. What on earth will the outcome of all this be?

The situation that the men find themselves in is clearly not ideal, and is not helped any by their continued 'incarceration', all be it at the hands of their victorious Russian Allies, rather than the German guards.

Parker's health is clearly not good, and although he outlines what he feels is the causation behind it, there is no clarity on his part whether he has sought medical treatment or advice, and if so, what it was that he was told by the camp's doctor. As for Jack, he is a good health-wise, or at least he is in a physical sense, but not being able to leave the camp and go it on his own took its toll on him. But this was a reaction not just to this one situation, but his overall frustration at nothing having really happened since they had become separated from their German guards and fully liberated when Russian forces over ran their location on their way to Germany.

Wednesday 21 February 1945

Severe diarrhea [*sic*] again this morning. I felt horribly sick and weak. Kept laying down, but had of necessity to get up and make little excursions to the lavatory frequently, each time feeling weaker and more sick.

Mac told me that the only thing to do was to keep off food altogether until the attack had passed. This is not too difficult to do after one look at the stew, but I feel very hungry. I felt a little stronger in the evening and got up, heated some water on the fire and had a good wash down. I took a little dry toast and a drink and went back to bed where I read by candlelight until I felt tired enough to drop off to sleep.

There were rumours in plenty about the progress of the war today. The main ones concerned the fighting in the Far East and were to the effect that our combined fleets were 'showing their coat tails' up and down the coast of the Japanese mainland and that American forces were just twenty miles off Manilla. No one knows where these items of news come from. One just hears them; inevitably they get garbled and distorted by word of mouth and repetition and it does not do to place very much credence upon them.

There is still no news regarding our moving further homeward and we are still waiting. We are all getting to hate that word and all it stands for.

Thursday 22 February 1945

Once again we were duty platoon and consequently our morning was taken up with peeling potatoes, a disagreeable and dirty job. We were not called upon for any further fatigues, however, and the rest of the day was our own to do with as we liked, as if there was anything to do with it except wish it was over and consequently one day nearer to getting home.

I drew two more books from the library. I can get up to four at a time as none of the others bother with it and I can draw in their names.

Bob and Mac were both out as per usual this afternoon but they returned about half-past six with some 'loot' and we had a treat. This was real 'high tea' consisting of pancake on top of the stove which, if not particularly tasty, will be at least filling for a time.

Today's rumours state that one thousand released British prisoners of war left Lublin en route to Iran and that the entire Stalag XXA column has been taken by Russian troops.

Saturday 24 February 1945

Morning the same as all the other mornings here; get up, tidy the room, roll call, room inspection, dinner, tea, supper, bed. That doesn't sound so bad, perhaps, but the meals are such in name only, we are continually hungry, and the deadly monotony coupled with the uncertainty and killing inactivity is enough to drive you spotty at times.

We simply could not face the stew at dinner time so we lashed out and had boiled egg, flapjacks, bread and coffee. This practically cleaned out our meagre supplies but it made a nice change and we considered it well worth the expense. It was a wonderful feeling to be able to spurn the glutinous mess of barley and potatoes for once.

We still have no further news regarding getting out of this accursed hole and our detachment is being depleted daily by men making their own way or just taking up residence with friendly civilians. Jack talks a great deal about going on our own and Bob and Mac listen attentively and appear to agree with the idea. I am dead against it, however, and do not think I should attempt it. I feel that having been here this long it would be a mistake to leave because we are surely bound to move on soon. Then too, I would not like to roam around among these Russians trusting to luck not to run afoul of them. But most of all I feel that it would be foolhardy for the simple reasons that we have no idea where to make for to contact British authorities, we do not know how far it would be or in which direction, and we have no map. These seem unanswerable arguments to me. As long as we remain here with a reasonably large body we have some claim, however slight, to official recognition.

Dry bread and coffee for tea and then just nothing to do but to go to bed. The killing despair of this place is getting increasingly hard to bear. Something will give if the strain is not eased.

Sunday 25 February

We decided this morning that it was useless to hoard the little of cache of food that Jack had brought from Stalag XXA against a move that seems no nearer now than it did weeks ago. Accordingly we broke into 'iron rations' and had elevenses of bread and cheese washed down with a drink of good hot Ovaltine. How good these English things tasted!

This morning 'Tubby' Fulton addressed the parade and re-emphasised the futility of trying to make a go of it alone. I think Jack has given up his ideas, temporarily; although if we go on like this much longer, I believe he will revive them.

As a change from the ever present barley stew today we had mashed potatoes and pea gravy and ate to sufficiency. Our sugar is exhausted as is the spread and we are now reduced once more to dry bread. Another crisis has broken on us, the coal is exhausted too. And the weather is still far too cold to be without warmth in the room. Consequently we are starting to break up old furniture to burn. Indeed some of it is not so old. We have already stripped the shelves out of the cupboard and burned some perfectly sound chairs. As long as there is wood around in any shape or form we shall keep our fires going!

Each day here is just the one before and the dream of going home is fast fading into the obscurity of an unforeseeable future that it was for us in our Prisoner of War Camps.

Monday 26 February 1945

Heavy rainfall this morning and weather cold and miserable. Despite these conditions, however, Bob set off this morning to walk to Alexandrowo and back and was gone all day, returning at about eight o'clock this evening.

We still have a little cheese left for our bread and some Marmite which, although very salty and doubtless would be much better for use as hot drinks, certainly helps the bread down. The stews are as bad as ever, barley, potatoes and a little meat. The cooks are toying with the idea of saving a day's meat ration and serving us a 'dry' dinner every other day consisting of mashed potatoes, some sort of vegetable and a piece of meat and gravy and, if flour permits, a dumpling. On alternate days we would have boiled barley with sugar. I think this would be a vast improvement to the round of stew, stew, stew! I never want to see barley again as long as I live when I get home.

It was clear to see that prisoners of war, no matter what circumstances they were in, were so greatly affected by food, or rather the lack of it, that it became a major focus of their very existence. It was no doubt the number one thing that they dreamt of every night they slept, and thought about for every second they were awake the following day.

Tuesday 27 February 1945

Duty platoon again today. While we were spud peeling the results of the current Three Power Conference was read out to us. The Russians had given us a copy of the radio report and it certainly made good hearing. They seem to have everything settled for the post war period. How great it sounded to hear, after five years of German propaganda, what our people were going to do with Germany. We only hope that they will bring it home to the Jerries in no uncertain terms that they are going to pay dearly for all the misery and suffering they have caused. I don't think there will be any champions for leniency towards the Germans among the ex-prisoners of war.

Bob got round his friends in the cookhouse to allow him to use the stove and made some flour and water pancakes for elevenses. These we washed down with unsweetened coffee. By the time we had finished them it was 'Stew Up' and we overcame our repugnance and ate a plateful each.

This afternoon a party returned from Thorn with good news. They had apparently contacted a Russian Railway Transport Officer there and he told them that four thousand British ex-prisoners of war are in Odessa waiting to embark and as soon as they have done so we shall move to an assembly point, be made up to strength and then proceed to that port as the next party for repatriation. And all this possibly within the next three to ten days. Our spirits soared at this news and an air of great excitement swept through the whole camp. I don't mind saying that I prayed that this might come true before I went to bed. We have had so many, many disappointments in the past. If only it comes off this time. Everyone is full of this news; we can hardly get to sleep for thinking about it. Three to ten days, what's that. It'll soon pass! We have been so long here now that a few more days won't be noticed. Roll On!!!

Wednesday 28 February 1945

Despite Jack's optimistic predictions, that he made on 5 February 1945, that we would be home by that date, we are still here in Ciechocinek and no closer to England now than we were that night. However, everyone is feeling a little more chipper owing to last night's news. Personally I have a great hope of moving soon and I pray this is not ill founded optimism.

Bob and Mac were out this evening so Jack and I had tea alone of German soup powder, bread and sweetened coffee.

After we had finished, Maxwell came in for a chat. During the course of the evening he offered to sell for us the curtains hanging at our windows. These were made of a heavy cloth which he said the Poles would make in to clothing. He said he would rig us up a blackout curtain to take their place and, although we knew he would make a handsome profit for himself, whatever we got would be sheer profit. They weren't our curtains! We told him we would consult Bob and Mac when they returned and give him our answer in the morning,

Turned in before the two Scottish wanderers returned.

The dinner today was incomplete. It needed straws to drink it through! But we are promised the first of the new 'dry' dinners tomorrow.

News item that appeared from nowhere today:- Dussledorf has fallen and a big new offensive opened on the Western Front by the British and Americans.

Chapter Six

The Diary of Leonard J. Parker – Part Three: March 1945

Thursday 1 March 1945

March lived up to its reputation and came in like a lion. It was very gusty, wet and extremely unpleasant outdoors, all day.

Bob and Mac agreed wholeheartedly to Maxwell's proposition to sell our curtains and he accordingly put us up a screen of black out paper to comply with regulations and pushed off with the curtains promising to get us the best price he could, in food of course.

Captain Lake addressed us on parade and confirmed the latest news that we move in the next few days and shall go home by sea via Odessa, the Black Sea port, in all probability.

Dinner was a little better today; it consisted of potatoes, gravy and two very small dumplings. At least it was far more palatable than boiled barley.

Maxwell brought the proceeds of the sale to us after dinner, a few eggs, a pat of butter and some bacon. Fair enough! We shall have a bit of decent food for a while and all it has cost us is a pair of curtains. At all events, it has cost somebody a pair of curtains. But, 'Ya gotta live'.

Washed some kit this afternoon and then we had a tea of meat sandwiches and sweet coffee. We discussed the possibilities of an imminent move this afternoon until about eight o'clock when we supped off some tasty bacon fat sandwiches and more coffee.

Hung my washing up to dry when everyone was out of the way in bed and then turned in myself. We are feeling a little more optimistic now; the news is better and we have a little extra food. It's amazing what a difference this latter makes!

The war news was good today, if true: it was that the Western Allies have crossed the Rhine and captured several towns. Now the Jerries are really playing on their home ground for the first time and I bet they don't like it one little bit.

Slept fairly well tonight despite a coldness in my bed.

Friday 2 March 1945

Snowfall during the night and weather still blustery and cold when we woke up this morning.

Another dry and more satisfying dinner today which we followed with a fairly decent tea of pancakes and custard, there having been an issue of flour today.

I almost blush to record it, but the curtains will soon be entirely eaten. We will think it was not a bad deal.

A fairly weak rumour made the usual rounds today of a move tomorrow and although I am inclined to doubt it, still I have a strong feeling, a kind of hunch I guess, that our stay in Ciechocinek is drawing to a close at long last. I certainly do hope so.

The Library has been open twelve days today and I have been one of its best customers. I find that in twelve days I have read sixteen books; pretty good going I think, and a very varied assortment.

I enjoyed, even savoured, every word in every one of these books. They passed many an hour which would have otherwise been tedious and dreary. They were good friends.

Saturday 3 March 1945

A Russian Commission appeared this morning to have a look at us. Roll call was cancelled and we were ordered to tidy our billets and stand by for a tour of inspection.

This we did. We waited and waited, but the Russians did not put in an appearance on our side at all. Rumours were flying around like mad all the time they were here but it was not until after they had gone that we heard anything reasonably definite. Captain Lake carried out his usual inspection of rooms and when he reached us he gave us the information as he had from the Russian authorities. It was to the effect that within three to five days we entrain here with Odessa as our objective and that, once on our way, we shall have no halt longer than forty-eight hours at any point en route.

On the face of it all this sounds suspiciously like the usual line they have been giving us ever since we first landed at this place, which seems to have been years and years ago, but I have a sort of premonition about it this time. It may well be wishful thinking, but all the same there is a strong undercurrent of rising expectation among all the chaps and I personally cannot rid myself of the feelings that we are going to get a break at long last. Despite my efforts to take all rumours with the proverbial pinch of salt, I have built my hopes high of moving off not later than Thursday, which will be the fifth day. I could be wrong but somehow I don't think it will be. We shall see.

We had egg for tea again thanks to the curtains; bread and butter and ersatz coffee for supper then turned in.

The weather has turned wintry again and if we do move soon it will be a cold and uncomfortable journey. But we are more than willing to put up with that for the sake of getting out of this backwater and making tracks in the right direction.

Sunday 4 March 1945

THIS IS IT! After all these long a dreary weeks of waiting, waiting; of hopes built high and then dashed to earth; weeks of rumour, speculation, guessing; of frustration and despair; at long last we have been given our marching orders.

We have shaken the dust of Ciechocinek from our feet and are actually on our way homewards! There is a very long way to go, of course, but sufficient unto the day is the fact that we are moving. The horrible period of waiting is over and we are actually on the move. Thank God. At times we thought it would never come but here we are on the first leg of our journey.

What a day! After a seemingly endless period of inactivity, everything happened at once. And yet the day started off in the usual dull, monotonous way that all our days in Ciechocinek have started, with nothing to mark it as the Red Letter Day it has certainly turned out to be.

There was the inevitable routine of getting up, scratch breakfast, roll call and billet inspection. After the inspection Bob and Mac set off to walk back to Alexandrowo to attend a party to which they had been invited by their Polish friends, intending to stay there overnight and return tomorrow. It seems strange now that after having all the time in the world on our hands they would choose today of all days to push off like this. But of course they had no way of knowing that this was to be The Day.

Jack was busy on his own affairs and as it was our platoon's turn for baths I overcame my modesty and went over for a hot shower. The wash down we have in the room is good enough for a little while, but we have to have a proper bath occasionally even at the expense of flaunting our nudity to the female bath attendants' disinterested gaze. As usual they paid us no attention at all, but it is hard to ignore their presence when we are running around clothed in nothing but our blushes.

I had left the chaps settling down to yet another day of dull monotony but when I got back I was amazed to find the whole camp fairly seething with excitement. Everyone was bubbling over with the news and it was not difficult to get someone to tell me what it was all about. Apparently a convoy of Russian Army lorries had driven up the road and halted outside the billets. A driver hailed one of our chaps who was standing nearby and asked for the 'Anlichan

Kommandant.' That was enough! In a flash the word spread round. These lorries had come for us. This was the much discussed transport to take us to a railhead.

The move had come.

And sure enough, at 2:45 we were officially ordered to pack our kit and stand by to vacate billets at one hour's notice.

Jack and I were soon ready. We packed our valises, strapped our blankets around them, and put on the warmest clothing we had; this was going to be a cold business in the wintry weather now prevailing.

But what were we to do about Bob and Mac? They were seven miles away all unaware of the great event and there was no chance that they would come back of their own accord before morning. We simply had to get word to them somehow; we'd be gone by tomorrow and they would be left behind. Jack toyed with the idea of borrowing a bicycle and riding post haste to fetch them. But if he did that there was every likelihood that he too would get left and he decided against it. Finally, we hit on the idea of getting a Polish friend of Jack's to ride to Alexandrowo on his bike, find Bob and Mac and warn them of the turn of events. This was the best we could do. The only thing now was to pack their kit for them so that no time would be wasted if they got to us in time, and hope for the best. This we did, with everything ready to pick up at a moment's notice, Jack and I sat back, and cursed Bob and Mac roundly, but quite unjustifiably, for causing us this anxiety us this anxiety, and waited for the word to 'Go'.

The afternoon passed on wings of lead and darkness and fell with no further developments, and still no Bob and Mac. We wondered if our courier had been able to find them and if so, whether they would be able to get back before we left. The move might start any minute now, surely. We hoped they knew that it was quicker to leave the road and follow the railway lines from Alexandrowo to Ciechocinek. It was going to be a pretty close call if they were to make it.

About half-past seven, Wally Kersey and Johnny Gaskin came up to our room to chat and pass the time. We sat by our last fire which was burning merrily, fed by pieces of furniture for which we now had no further use. We were determined to have a good warm up; it might have to last us a long time. We had been talking for half an hour or so when suddenly the door opened and, Allah be praised, in walked Big Jock and Mac looking rather flustered, a little out of breath, and greatly relieved to find us still there. They had made it. I felt a weight off my mind as I had been pretty worried at the thought of losing them after being so long together. Jack too, I know, felt the same, but he immediately began to berate them. Bob gave him one of the famous Smith looks.

'Alright, alright,' he glowered. 'We're here. That's all that matters. Never mind the "I told you so's". We're here, Jack. Now shut up.'

Wally and Johnny, sensing a first class row in the making, made a strategical withdrawal. 'Your social flutters nearly cost you the boat, Smithy,' said Jack. And there was no denying that he was entirely right.

'I know, I know.' Bob was getting exasperated. He and Mac had a hectic time of it during the last few hours and were in no mood for baiting. 'But we made it ok. So that's that. Forget it. We're here. Shut up! Forget it.'

And forget it we did. We were both so very, very glad to see them and felt so relieved that we wouldn't have to leave them behind that nothing else mattered and we were only too willing to forgive them the very anxious hours we had endured waiting for them to get back.

Would this time never come? We sat and waited on tenterhooks. Was this to be yet another disappointment? Time wore on and we got more and more disheartened. Then almost as we were giving up hope and considering getting our heads down for the night, it came. A shrill blast on a whistle, the 'Fall In'. It was nearly midnight. Hurriedly we put on our greatcoats, hoisted each other's packs into position and made our way outside.

A roll call revealed that the whole detachment was present, with no exception. Here was a queer trick of fate. CSM Darley, that stoutest antagonist of leaving camp at any time, 'Doc' Darley who had exhorted us at every opportunity and at all times not to wander off, to stay close at hand so as to be 'on tap' for any developments and to obviate the risk of being left behind, had gone off early in the morning to walk to Thorn for the day. In consequence he had missed the move for which we had all waited so long. It was really tough luck, but there was nothing we could do about it.

We piled into the trucks, sixteen in each that would have held half that number with any degree of comfort. We were horribly cramped, it was bitterly cold and dark and snow had started to fall thickly. The lorries were covered with canvas roofs and sides which kept the snow off but afforded no protection against the cold; the wind whistled in the cracks and in a very few minutes we were all frozen to very marrow of our bones. There was the inevitable delay while forming up arrangements were made and then between half-past twelve and quarter to one, the convoy started up and began to roll. We were on the move.

It was truly a nightmare ride. The Russians were the world's worst drivers, crashing along the ice bound roads at terrific speeds with recklessness and complete disregard of safety, born either of great courage or sheer animal ignorance. Having seen quite enough of these people I was inclined to favour the latter explanation!

There was not even room enough to stamp our feet to keep the blood circulating. All we could do was sit, packed like sardines, and get colder and colder until we began to lose all sense of feeling in our feet, legs and hands. The lorry lurched and swayed sickeningly and the smell of exhaust fumes penetrated our tent-like shelter to add to the feeling of sickness and nausea. One chap was soon overcome, and vomited heartily on the floor and those nearest him with impartiality, and passed out. We stuck his head out in to the cold air and he quickly revived. That wind was kill or cure.

The night was filled with incident. The first of these occurred when we dashed full speed around a sharp curve which led on to a bridge over the Vistula. Suddenly the wheels of the lorry failed to get a grip on the hard packed snow and ice, we went in to a swift, gliding skid which turned us halfway round, and came to rest with a heavy thud with the rear end considerably lower than the front. We were all thrown about helter-skelter like peas in a drum, arms and legs flying and bodies crashing and falling over each other in a tangled mess of humanity. Slowly we sorted ourselves out, relieved to find there had been no casualties. Being near the back, I looked out to see what had happened. I felt a thrill of horror go all through me and the hairs on the back of my neck started to prickle. I was looking down, not onto solid earth, but into a deep chasm, down into the river. The truck had ended up with the front wheels still on the road but at right angles to our line of progress, while the back wheels were hanging over the edge of the river bank with nothing between them and the Vistula but thirty feet of thin air. We were in imminent danger of plunging down that steep slope to almost certain death. My mouth went dry; my stomach was having butterfly trouble again. No one dared move for fear of dislodging the truck from its precarious perch.

Our driver seemed quite unconcerned however. With no further ado he revved up his engine, engaged the front wheel drive, and with a great roaring and crashing of gears, the truck slowly moved forwards and upwards and slid back on to the road. In a few minutes we were once more on our way.

We stopped every hour or so for a very short spell and at one of these halts Jack moved up front with the driver, leaving his place to be shared equally between the fifteen of us. The next thing our capable, if somewhat erratic driver did was to lose the convoy. For an hour or more we sped along on our own while he tried to find the others. Finally he left the road and made his overland way through forests, over ploughed fields, up hills and across streams before he joined the main road once more and, more through luck than judgement, found the rest of the column just ahead of him.

As cold as I was and cramped almost beyond endurance, nature finally had her way and I slept. For the rest of the night, jolting and bouncing along, cold and miserable, I dozed fitfully until it was light.

Monday 5 March 1945

Dawn found us tired, hungry, frozen and suffering horribly from cramp and poor blood circulation, but still hurtling along the roads towards the entrainment point.

We had left the open country behind us now and were passing through villages and towns of considerable size. No one had the vaguest idea where we were. At about half-past seven our lorry, crowning touch, broke down completely and we had to transfer to another which had no hood or shelter of any kind. We finished the journey in this mobile refrigerator. Luckily, however, it was only for an hour or so.

At 8.30 we entered a large town, drove slowly through the streets, past a large freight yard where we could see trains and hundreds of freight cars busily shunting back and forth. This was a welcome sight. Finally we turned in to a driveway, passed through some large iron gates and pulled up on a huge parade ground. We had arrived.

How I ever got my limbs working again, I don't know. When I crawled off the truck violent shooting pains stabbed through my legs as the blood forced its way through again and I nearly fell to the ground, for my legs almost refused to support me. But some intense stamping and flapping of arms soon got the circulation started once more and we made our way in to the billets to which we had been assigned.

We learned that this was indeed the railhead; a town called Wreznia, Wreschen in German. We were in what had been a vast military barracks and was now being used as a collecting point for all nationalities of released prisoners of war, British, American, French, Belgian and Russian. There were literally thousands of them here, some of them had been waiting for weeks. But we understood that we British and the Americans who had come with us from Ciechocinek were to make up a detachment which would be the next to leave. We certainly hoped so.

We were extremely hungry, so we made a hot drink of sorts and had a bite to eat from our meagre rations. This was soon finished and we squared up our kit and settled down to wait for further orders.

We waited until half-past four in the afternoon when we were called on parade and told that we would not be going off until tomorrow morning. So back to the billet we went to make ourselves as comfortable as possible until then. We managed to scrounge some coal, got straw in and spread it on the floor, so we shall be fairly warm. By contrast to the truck it is a heaven of comfort to stretch out and have a bit of warmth.

Bob boiled up some water on the stove and made a drink of hot Marmite which we had together with some dry toast. The Russians gave us no food whatsoever. But we were too exhausted to worry much about anything else and we soon collapsed on to the straw, drew our blankets over us and pounded the ear.

It was pitch dark when I awoke to hear the crash of anti-aircraft guns. I looked at my watch; it was three o'clock. A veritable thunder of firing broke out as I lay there listening. Heavy Ack Ack, rifle fire, pistol shots even. All manner of guns were going off in a deafening fusillade. Even the sentry who was on duty outside our billet was pointing his rifle into the air and firing for all he was worth. The night sky was criss-crossed with tracer and lit by scarlet flashes of fire, shrapnel whined and whistled all around and crashed onto roofs and concrete roads. There was no shelter to be had. All we could do was to lay there and hope for the best. The noise continued until daylight broke and we got only snatches of sleep,

We are building up our spirits on moving off in the morning and if we have to stay here for any length of time it will be a horrible anti-climax to our hopes. I don't think many of us could stand any protracted delays now.

We are now on Russian daylight savings time and those of us who have not yet had our watches stolen by our hosts, have put them ahead two hours.

Tuesday 6 March 1945

Slept through until half-past eight and then washed and repacked. On enquiry we learned that last night's firing had been on account of two German planes which had been reported as being 'somewhere in the vicinity'. The Russians, however, would not wait until the aircraft could be spotted, or even heard, but forthwith opened up with everything they could muster and continued doing so until daylight. The German planes had not once been sighted but our Russian friends evidently considered an ounce of prevention to be worth a pound of ammunition. Certainly nothing could have survived that terrific hail of fire. The Russians must have more ammo than sense, I think.

The snow had stopped falling by the time we had got up, but it was still bitterly cold and a sharp wind cuts through you like a knife. We were told that the train is packed with six days rations and is ready and waiting for us on a siding in the goods yards. We were not kept waiting too long for the order to fall in. When it came we made our way down to the huge parade ground and stood about while lists were checked and counter checked, objects of great interest to the French who are apparently staying here for some time yet. Thank heavens we are not.

When all was in readiness the Americans were the first to form up. They made a good show of it; well-disciplined and smart in their drill movements. We all felt a sense of responsibility. The British were in the minority here and it was up to us to show everyone that, despite five years of imprisonment, we could still hold our end up in a display of smartness. At the words of command we sprang sharply to attention, marched on to the square in good order, down past the waiting ranks of Americans until we drew abreast of their leading files and then with two sharply defined crashing stamps, halted and stood at ease. With every single chap on his mettle we had put on a show which would not have disgraced a troop of well-drilled soldiers straight off the barrack square. The Americans broke out in to spontaneous cheering; one shouted, 'Nice going fellows. Still in good style.' We felt pleased with ourselves.

It is interesting to note how much it meant to these men to present themselves on parade as best they possibly could, despite the fact that many of them had been in captivity for some five years. They might not have seen much in the way of active service after their early capture in the war, but they still had a pride in the appearance and their ability to perform, even if it was only on the parade square.

As an appreciation of the fact that we had been prisoners for so very long, the American Colonel had requested that we should have the honour of leading the column. Mac, Bob and I were the three leading files of the British contingent and so it was that we marched at the head of the entire body; it was indeed a wonderful sensation. Out through the big iron gates, down the road and right through the middle of town we marched, watched with great interest by civilians and Russian soldiers. It was a grey, damp day, but our spirits were high and we all marched with a will, swinging our arms in regulation style and stamping our feet down on the cobble stoned streets.

It was clear to see what the relatively straightforward task of marching in a controlled environment meant to these men. This was despite the fact that the war for them had long since been over, and here they were preparing for their journey back home, but still they wanted to be well thought of by their fellow prisoners of war. It provided them with a feeling of self-respect, something which many of them had very rarely had the opportunity to achieve during their many years of enforced captivity as prisoners of the Germans.

It was not a very long way to the goods yard and we were soon there. We made our way across tracks, past railway wagons of all kinds until finally we came to a long train of box cars which stood waiting for us. After the usual period of standing around and waiting, we were detailed off into sections and scrambled in to the box cars to which we had been allocated. There were sixty in each eight wheeled truck; inside there had been placed two small stoves, one at each end, and a series of tiers had been constructed, each of which held six of us. On these we placed straw mattresses so that, with our blankets and greatcoats we shall be fairly warm, albeit a little cramped. We soon settled ourselves in and fell to wondering how long it would be before an engine was coupled on and we would be moving.

After an hour or so a stew was issued. It was the usual conglomeration of barley, potatoes and a microscopic portion of meat, but we were hungry and ate heartily. Everyone was cheerful and eager to be on our way. It was getting colder as night drew in, and we lit a fire in the stove and banked it up with some coal which had 'appeared' and it was quite snug. Time dragged on and we were still at a standstill. It had been an exciting day and we felt tired, and so gradually the chaps turned in, sliding themselves with great difficulty in to the low shelves which served as our beds. At last there was only Bob, I left awake and we sat by the little stove determined to be on tap if and when the train should pull out.

Soon after midnight there was a sudden crash and our truck lurched backwards and Bob and I nearly fell to the floor. The engine had been coupled on, and at 12:20, with a series of spine whacking jerks, clankings and bangings, the train started to move forward, slowly at first as we passed over the points and crossings of the freight yards, and then with increasing speed as we cleared them and got on to the tracks which led eventually to our destination. Bob and I watched the lights of houses and trains out of the tiny slit high up on the side of our truck until we could hardly stand any longer.

I wrote up my diary by the light of a stump of a candle, although it was a very jerky business, and then turned in.

There was none too much room, crammed in between Mack and Jack, but I was tired and I slept soundly, despite the swaying lurching and banging which never seemed to lessen.

Wednesday 7 March 1945

Slept very soundly but heavily and awoke at half-past seven to a cup of coffee which was at least warm and wet. There is no water to wash in and getting up consists merely of crawling out of our shelves and standing up on our feet.

The train had slowed down considerably and was crawling along through snow covered countryside and through small towns and villages, which had been blasted by the battles fought through them. There was much of interest to see but not more than three at the most could crowd round the tiny slits and the rest had to content themselves with sitting round on the floor and talking.

At half-past nine the train stopped all together to permit us to have a toilet break and to receive a ration of food. We each got a ladleful of watery soup and a loaf of bread which we were told must last us for three days. When we had eaten this bountiful meal the engine gave a series of warning toots and we were again on the move. We could really have walked quicker than the train and it was hard to be patient while proceeding at a snail's pace. It is understandable, however. The entire system of tracks has had to be relaid to conform to the Russian gauge, and in addition, the signalling system is completely destroyed and all trains have to be hand signalled. For miles on end there is only a single line; we wonder what will happen if we meet a train going the other way? Not a thought on which to dwell.

Stopped again from noon to one o'clock for no apparent reason. Moved off slowly again; we seem to be heading east. One of the chaps in the truck has a map and we frequently consult this, checking the names of any town through which we pass and can see a name board. Our guess is that we are heading towards Warsaw.

Made yet another stop this afternoon and our truck was put on fatigues, fetching water from a nearby well for the boilers in the cook wagon. The train was on the top of a steep bank and we had to scramble down to the well at the bottom. We lost several buckets trying to manage the long hooked pole onto which we had to fasten our pails and dip for water. The pails kept slipping off when we poked them down the well and at least three sunk to the bottom for every one we contrived to fill and bring up to the surface again.

In the middle of this fishing for water, the engine suddenly made tentative moving noises and indeed the train actually started to roll. Down went pole, bucket and all, and we dashed like mad up the bank and were hauled quickly into the truck by willing hands. No sooner had we got in than the train stopped again, having moved only a few yards. We finished our fatigues, but kept a very watchful eye on the engine. We were taking no chances of being stranded.

Made very little progress for the rest of the day; we kept stopping for long periods and then moving very slowly on again. At half-past seven a meal was issued, soup, and we found it quite satisfying with a chunk of bread and a cigarette to follow.

The weather is bitterly cold and our very small stock of coal is exhausted. We have been running through extremely heavy snowfalls and the truck is soaking wet from the snow brought in our boots. The only thing to do is to lie on our shelves under our blankets and huddle together to keep warm.

The quarters are horribly cramped and the chaps are quickly getting browned off. The interminable halts do not help our frayed tempers. Everyone is fed up to the teeth and it is to be hoped that we do not have to put up with these conditions for very long.

Thursday 8 March 1945

We had been moving when I fell asleep last night, but this morning I awoke to find that we have been in freight yards outside Warsaw since three o'clock. Climbed out of the truck and had a wash of sorts in the snow. Bitterly cold, and the snow numbed my fingers and left me gasping for breath when I dashed it on my face. Melted some down on the stove, which was burning fitfully with some bits of wood we had scrounged, and had a shave. Felt much refreshed for these ablutions.

Cleaned our truck out as best we could and straightened up our kit. At least it kept us occupied and it is better to be doing something rather than sitting around chafing on our delays.

The Russians opened their hearts this morning and issued us with some blocks of compressed tea. This we crumbled up and stewed in a bucket of water. With a little sugar it was quite palatable and the nearest thing to a decent drink we have had for many days. In addition we were given a little sugar, and in lieu of a morning soup, we got one tin of lard between ten men. This was very welcome as we have long felt the need of some fat; Bob sliced up some bread, toasted it on the stove and we tucked in to toast and lard. It went down well.

We did not travel at all today, but spent the entire day in three cursed freight yards. They seem determined that we shall have a good look at every freight yard from here to Odessa; as soon as we see one ahead we try to resign ourselves to another long hold up.

Although I am sure there was a very good reason for these numerous stops, it must have been extremely frustrating for the British prisoners of war to have to endure, especially if every time they did stop, they were not provided with an explanation as to why. By now, all these men wanted was to get back home to their families, with many of them having been in captivity for nearly five years.

A barley stew was forthcoming for dinner and although it tasted vile it blew us up for a few hours.

One of the chaps found a huge pile of railroad sleepers nearby and we raided it and got away with a few before the

Russian guards spotted us and drove us off at bayonet point. Apparently these sleepers are used as fuel for the engines. We are more interested in getting a bit of warmth into our chilled bones than in the running of the Russian engines, however. Happily, someone left a buck saw unattended for a few moments and it soon found its way in to our truck. We shall saw up the logs only while the train is moving, otherwise the guard would hear the noise and take the saw away from us.

Trains started up at half-past ten tonight and puffed along slowly with only a few stops during the night. As soon as we were under way we got the saw out, cut up some wood and built a fire. The warmth felt good and put fresh heart in us.

We were told that we may be anything up to ten days en route. The two days we have already spent in this cattle truck seem like two weeks. I don't know how we shall ever get through another week or so.

Friday 9 March 1945

Today is Bob's birthday. What a place to have to spend it, jammed in a cold, dirty freight wagon with 59 other chaps, hungry and miserable.

The weather is bitterly cold, but we have got our stove going and huddle around it as best we can. Those who cannot get near it remain under their blankets. We were given ten German cigars each today. They are exactly like brown paper, taste like burning roofing felt and smelt like garbage incinerators. But we smoke them!

One of the chaps in our truck found that he got lice today. I am not surprised. Under these conditions they are almost inevitable, but neither am I surprised at the particular chap who discovered them on himself. He has made no attempt whatsoever to freshen himself since we entrained and, indeed, all the time we were at Ciechocinek with facilities for washing and bathing, he was never even reasonably clean. I dare say he had them before we left Wreznia. I am glad that he is on the top shelf, well removed, at least as far as possible from the four of us on the bottom.

We reported the fact to our medical officer and he in turn to the Russian authorities who were not the least bit interested. They gave us nothing to ward off this threat. Luckily Mac had a small box of Keatings and we sprinkled this both on our bedding and ourselves. I only hope we manage to keep clear of livestock. It's a horrible feeling, and I have had quite enough of it in the past. What a birthday present for poor old Bob.

Our train, going down line as it is, must give precedence to those coming with supplies, equipment and troops for the front. Consequently we move in fits and starts and today, being no exception, we get shunted off in to a freight yard where we spent most of the day. The time dragged, there was nothing to do but just sit, wait and hope.

According to the best of our knowledge and such deductions as we can make by looking at the map, we are heading for Brest Litovsk. This is the frontier post between Poland and Russia and the only point, we are told, at which any crossing is allowed. The Russian officers who are travelling with us have said that once we get into Russia we shall make much better time to Odessa. I only hope that they are right. This stop and go system, more stop than go, is wearing.

I took advantage of the long halt today to melt some snow, strip to the waist and have as good a wash as I could manage. Felt much better for it and after a shave, things looked a little brighter. It's surprising how a clean-up makes one feel less downhearted.

Turned in late thinking we were due to stay here all night, but no sooner was I about to drop off to sleep than came the terrible crashing and jolting which always precedes getting under way and the train started off once more.

These freight cars were not meant to carry passengers and we have a rough ride of it. When lying in bed we seem to spend most of the time suspended between our own shelf and that immediately above us. There is no head room at all,

A cartoon from the booklet Happy Returns.

The inside cover of A Diary of Liberation.

A group of British PoWs posing for a photo at Stalag XXA.

A group of PoWs at the camp. Such images seem to have been quite common place.

A group photo of some of those held at Stalag XXA. All of whom look fit and healthy.

A photograph of Stalag XXA PoW camp.

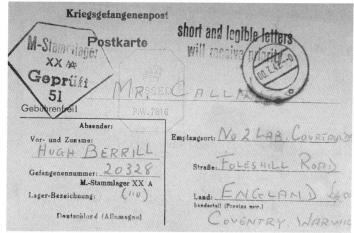

A postcard sent from Stalag XXA by Hugh Berrill to a Mr Callaghan in 1942.

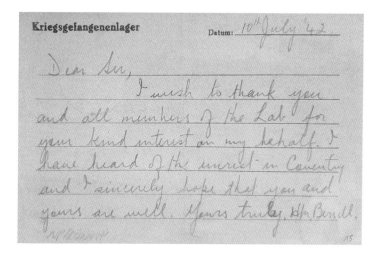

The message sent in the postcard from Hugh Berrill.

Above: *A postcard sent to Mr and Mrs Barringer from Horace Briar.*

Left: *The rear of the above postcard sent to Mr and Mrs Barringer. Horace Briar is one of those in the photograph.*

A boxing match between PoWs. One of the camp's many sporting events.

A group of British PoWs at Stalag XXA, in what appears to be some kind of a changing room.

BSM WOll 791318 Edwin Gardner Royal Artillery. He was a POW at both Stalag 383 and Stalag XXA.

It wasn't only the PoWs who liked having their photograph taken; so did the camp guards.

" WISDOM MUST BE SOUGHT."
— YOUNG.

Some of the camp's PoWs taking the opportunity to improve their education in the classroom at Stalag XXA.

An organised football match taking place at the camp between some of the PoWs.

Funeral for a British PoW. The British sergeant facing the coffin is holding a peaked cap in his left hand.

Right: *The winter funeral of a Stalag XXA PoW is attended by some of his comrades.*

Below: *A group of PoWs at XXA in 1942. The man in the middle of the second row from the front is BSM Edwin Gardner.*

Above: *A group of unknown, relaxed looking PoWs at Stalag XXA.*

Left: *Some of the camp's more energetic PoWs engaging in Gymnastics.*

A letter addressed to Flying Officer A.W. Matthews, a camp PoW.

Dear Mother & Father, I am very pleased to say
that I have received your letter of April 2nd
& it is pleasing & encouraging to know that
both you & Dorothy are receiving my mail
in quick time. Dorothy told me in a letter
of your present to her for her birthday, hoping
that my letter reached you in which I asked

you to purchase Dorothy a present out of
my "dibs". I feel proud of Dorothy & I am sure
that I am lucky, after some of the news
that some of the boys here have received.
Remember me to Fred, Jack & Walter, thanking
Walter & family for their birthday greetings,
also Doris, Nellie, & my Aunt. To whom ....
.... me all happy
I have two good pals, Bob & Albert by
name, I mentioned them in a previous letter
& by the way they eventually persuaded
me to do a short spell in the garden, & I
enjoyed it very much. It may interest you to
know that 'Pop' Heywood as passed the
board for home &   .... ation commences.
.... seems a   I do not worry

Right: *A letter from a PoW at the camp to his parents in the UK.*

Below: *PoWs in the library at Stalag XXA.*

Some of the camp's PoWs taking full advantage of the monthly bath time.

Above left: *The PoW ID tag of BSM Edwin Gardner.*

Above right: *The identity tag of an unknown PoW.*

Kriegsgefangenenlager   Datum 2-3-41

Dear Sir, I thank you for your letter dated 20th Nov. 1940 which I received on the 20th Feb 1941. I am in the best of health. I would be very pleased if you would write to my mother in England the address is 9 Priory Rd Ramsgate Kent. We are allowed to have mags and food parcels sent us and clothes. I would be very pleased indeed with anything. Thanking you once again, Sincerely yours, F. Dale

The message sent by PoW Private Fred Dale in his postcard to the USA.

PoW Private Fred Dale sent a postcard to an address in the USA, asking the recipient to write to his mother in Ramsgate, Kent, explaining he was ok.

Above left: *A group of 4 unknown PoW's at Stalag XXA.*

Above right: *Believed to be a pre-war photo of a Stalag XXA PoW. The back of the photo says 17 May 1943, Ken.*

Left: *A scene from one of many of the shows put on at Stalag XXA.*

The rather cramped sleeping arrangements at Stalag XXA, especially if there were any snorers in the group.

Above left: *Souvenir booklet issued to released PoWs who travelled back to the UK on board the SS* Duchess of Richmond.

Above right: *Sport platz at fort 15. The athletics track is clearly marked out.*

SS Duchess of Richmond, *the ship that took home the released PoWs.*

Above left: *The camp's tailor, hard at work.*

Above right: *The plain front cover of* A Diary of Liberation *by Leonard Parker, on which this book is based on.*

Left: *A group of four unknown PoWs posing for a photograph.*

Above: *PoWs on stage for one of the camp's many shows.*

Right: *At many of the bigger PoW camps, such as Stalag XXA, the British Free Corps made attempts to recruit new members.*

Below: *Funeral Service at Stalag XXA for a British PoW.*

Above: *Outdoor band practice.*

Left: *An aerial photograph of the camp.*

The camp's PoWs who were below the rank of sergeant were expected to work and become part of an Arbeitskommando Labour Unit. This was the type of ID card they would have had.

the shelf above being only about two feet higher than ours, and we are continually cracking our heads as we get in and out. We get tossed around mercilessly as the train bumps along and it is a wonder that we get any sleep at all. The engine driver is a terror. When he starts off he simply throws the throttle wide open, the driving wheels spin frantically until they grip the rails, all the trucks are hurled against each other with terrific force and we are flung to the floor if we happen to be standing up or, if we are lying down, we are bounced off the boards into the air and have to ward ourselves off the shelf above to prevent ourselves being hurled bodily against it. Then we crash onto our own shelf again where we lie waiting for the next series of bangings. Most of us are quite heavily bruised; nearly everyone has got at least one or two quite nasty bumps as a result of this continual jolting. We shan't be at all sorry to get off this jumping cracker box.

Saturday 10 March 1945

Awoke in still another freight yard this morning. Don't know how long we have been here, but I hope we don't stay long.

Both breakfast and dinner today consisted of Russian dried tea brewed up on the stove and dry bread. We're getting hungry again now. The rations the Russians give us are totally inadequate and as tasteless and nauseous as those which the Germans provided in camp. But what makes it even more galling is the fact that we see Russian soldiers gorging themselves on American canned foods in plenty, none of which comes to us. The only rations we get are captured food dumps of barley and bread.

This junction is at Siedlice, halfway between Warsaw and Brest Litovsk which is the frontier station. Apparently we arrived here at about 3:30 am and here we stopped all day. A troop train passed through on its way up to the front, packed to bursting with men, wireless trucks, lorries, petrol, goods wagons, tanks and guns.

The weather is still very cold and it is getting colder as we go on. Snow is very heavy and the scenery becomes more wild and desolate as we approach the frontier. We learned that there was a large Italian Stalag here when the Germans were in occupation. How they ever stood the cold beats me. I expect most of them just didn't!

We finally pulled out about 5 o'clock, and stopped again at 6 o'clock. Drew out at 11 and stopped again at 12. This went on throughout the night until we finally stopped altogether at 3 am. This stop and go method of travelling doesn't cover much ground. Out of yesterday's twenty-four hours, we were actually on the move for only one and a half. It would be quicker to walk, and yet we can do nothing except sit and chafe at the delays. Everyone's spirits go up when we are moving, but at each stop tempers are short and the chaps are all downhearted again.

We had another fat issue today, 4 to a tin, so we need not eat dry bread for a bit, which latter, even, is none to plentiful.

Sunday 11 March 1945

Halted again during the night. Awoke to find ourselves in the inevitable goods yard drawn up alongside a Russian hospital train thickly coated with snow and frost. It is very cold indeed, and takes a lot of courage to perform our necessary ablutions and toilet alongside the train.

Breakfast was unusual, thick pudding, and barley with a dash of meat in it. A few mouthfuls of this was sufficient to blow us out like balloons but the effect was soon gone and we were hungry again.

We moved off again at 11:45 this morning and were on the go until 5 o'clock when we pulled in to the freight yards of Brest Litovsk where we are able to cross from Poland in to the USSR. This area is horribly devastated and in every direction, as far as they eye can see, the raw wounds of bitter fighting give sufficient testimony to the ravages which the two campaigns have wrought. As we crossed the River Bug on a temporary bridge this afternoon we could see the remains of the original bridge which was blown by the retreating Germans. Great masses of twisted steel had been strewn about like straws in the wind and a huge locomotive lay on its side halfway down the bank looking like a toy train which had been flung down. Far below in the river another was half buried in the mud and all around were wrecked freight cars, torn up rails and burnt out tanks, trucks and spiked guns. A terrible scene.

Shortly after we halted we were issued with another stew which, repulsive as it was, we managed to shove down. At least it was warm.

These freight yards were full of activity. Gangs of Russian women, wrapped in sacking and weird varieties of heavy clothing against the cold were busy re-laying lines and repairing the damage to signalling systems, points and rolling stock. Long trains were loaded with materials for the front awaiting their turn to be hauled off. Our own locomotive is always used when we are at a standstill; they cannot afford to let one stand idle.

There were some Rumanian gypsies nearby and they clamoured round us begging for cigarettes and titbits. We had little or nothing to give them, but one, a mere child, suddenly appeared stark naked and proceeded to do a fantastic dance in the snow. Someone gave her a cigarette and she seemed to be entirely satisfied.

Further along the yard some Russians had got out their musical instruments and were playing for the amusement of onlookers. Russian men and women soldiers danced together between the tracks and shouted amiably to us to join them. Our chaps were more than happy to oblige and a good time was had by all.

We hope soon to be on our way again, but the cookhouse trucks have had their roofs blown off by a high wind and we must wait for them to be repaired. Turned in and slept fairly well.

Jack, continuing his eternal quest for souvenirs, palled up with a Russian Lieutenant today and persuaded him to give up his hammer and sickle cap badge.

Monday 12 March 1945

Awoke late this morning to find that we are still in the freight yards of Brest Litovsk with some 500 miles still between us and Odessa. Rations issued consisted of one loaf each of black bread, one tenth of a tin of meat and half a teaspoonful of sugar per man.

We spent a miserable day being shunted back and forth in the freight yards and began to think we were due for another night here. But finally the word buzzed around that we were to pull out. The engine backed on to our train and coupled up. But we were doomed to disappointment; the set of points which led from our siding back on to the main line, suddenly broke down and we were marooned. This wasted another couple of hours and it was not until 2:45, after 21 hours wait, that we finally pulled out and threaded our way through the maze of trains, across the frontier and on our way. As we drew away from Brest Litovsk, I saw a group of German civilians being herded along to work, heavily guarded by Russian soldiers and looking abject and miserable as our chaps must have looked in the early days of our confinement.

We had two fairly good bursts of speed along a single track with loop lines for passing. Of course we go on to the loops and everything else takes precedence over us. The architecture of the few buildings left standing shows clearly the Russian influence, with mosque like towers and spires. But the whole area is horribly scarred; bridges are blown up, houses burned to the ground with only a solitary chimney here and there and a pile of rubble to mark where once stood homes, churches and shops. There is much of interest to see and as the weather is somewhat milder, we opened the door of our truck and had a good view of the countryside.

Our fairly rapid progress was too good to last however, and after about 47 kilometres we stopped once more and stayed put. I took advantage of the halt to have a wash and to rinse out my under vest in the water to freshen it up a little. The small wayside station at which we had pulled up boasted a lavatory, the first we had met since leaving Ciechocinek. It was pretty fully booked, but I managed to get in, a welcome change from our usual practice of having to do the best we could alongside the train.

As night was drawing in our train moved on again and we kept up a pretty good pace throughout the night. These long, uninterrupted runs certainly do cover the ground and we are all tremendously bucked to think we are getting well on our way. Slept quite soundly despite the lurching, swaying and crashing which we endure all the time we are on the go. We had picked up a few logs at Brest Litovsk and consequently are able to keep our little stove burning.

Tuesday 13 March 1945

Weather milder again today and we made much better progress than usual, covering nearly 100 miles to Kovel where we arrived about noon. We literally tremble at the approach of each siding and breathe a sigh of relief when we pass one. But inevitably we stopped at dinner time and were issued with cement like barley stew. Here as everywhere else, desolation and ruin are to be seen on all sides. The station in which we halted was absolutely wrecked. It seemed as if there were not two bricks left in their original positions. The bridges, platforms and station buildings had been blown sky high and only a few smoke blackened timbers marked their one time boundaries.

A rumour flashed round today to the effect that we shall reach Odessa in 40 hours, by next Thursday, the Kiev route having been abandoned in favour of a more direct one, we hope so.

At this stop the local civilians set up a market for such kit as the chaps had. As we are in the Ukrainian wheat district, bread, oats and buns seem to be fairly plentiful and can be bought for money. Blankets are most in demand and fetch from 250, 300 roubles, and other things in proportion. Things were going with a swing; blankets were changing hands rapidly and the chaps were cashing in their roubles for foodstuffs immediately. It was too good to last however. The Russian authorities claimed quite without justification, that the blankets were not ours to sell, and the American officer in charge Colonel Fuller, put an embargo on all further trading and threatened to charge anyone who disobeyed his order. This was bitterly resented by all but in particular the British element. Most of us had brought our blankets all the way from Stalag XXA with us and considered it no one else's business if we now decided to flog them. But orders are orders and the market closed down, pro tem!

The boilers from the cookhouse wagons were transferred to others, the damaged roofs proving to be quite irreparable, and we were promised a stew as soon as all was once more in working order. Bob and I stayed up until midnight but the food did not materialise. We consoled ourselves with the thought that our journey must soon be coming to its end and crawled into bed, hungry but not too downcast.

We left Kowel about 2 o'clock in the afternoon and made good progress. During the afternoon we saw one of the countless hundreds of American trucks we had passed, the first British one, a Leyland. Jack was very interested to see at one point about two miles from the railway, a gigantic crucifix which looked horribly out of place among the ruins of a small town.

During the Second World War, after Nazi Germany had invaded Poland and the Soviet Union as part of Operation Barbarossa, they murdered 18,000 Jews in Kovel. Most of these mass killings were carried out during the months of August and September 1942. There had been a Jewish ghetto in Kovel since 25 May 1942, and another in the suburbs of Pyaski. In total they accounted for 24,000 Jews. Not one of them escaped execution by the Nazis.

The German 5th Panzer Division Viking, which meant it consisted of foreign nationals who had decided to fight for Nazi Germany instead of their own country against them, and the Soviet Union's Red Army, fought a vicious battle at Kovel during March and April 1944.

Later in the spring of 1944, some 3,700 Polish inhabitants of Kovel were murdered by Ukranian nationals. When post-war Europe was split up by the major powers, Kovel became part of the Ukranian Soviet Social Republic and the entire Polish population was forcibly resettled.

When Leonard Parker and his comrades arrived in the city on their route home, they would have not have had the slightest inclination about its murky secrets and the atrocities that had been carried out there.

Many of the places through which we pass are familiar names of the Russian campaign, and today we saw Rowno which had figured largely in our news bulletins in Kinheit Drei. We never thought then when we heard about them that one day we would actually see them. But here we are. We pulled up at 7 o'clock in the evening and were issued with five cigars each, German manufacture and just as vile as the last lot we had, but the air is thick with the smoke from them.

As I have already noted, Bob and I ended our wait for a stew and midnight and turned in and at about 1:30 am we were awakened by the crashing which heralds a move and fell asleep again with the happy thought that we were pushing on, and that the boat was getting nearer.

Wednesday 14 March 1945

The train climbed steadily this morning for three or four hours until it seemed as if we were never going to get to the top. The scenery was magnificent, endless vistas or rolling wheat fields stretching as far as the eye could see; thousands and thousands of acres of grain swaying in the breeze and looking for all the world like a vast golden sea. Then the ground levelled off and we coasted for an hour or so downhill into the valley and the train stopped on a loop line. Here we stayed while another stew was issued and then we were surprised to see that a second engine had appeared. This was coupled on behind and with one locomotive pulling and the other pushing, we started off once more, climbing up and up all the time.

Jack nearly got left behind. The train started off while he was wandering around outside, and he only just managed to scramble aboard one of the trucks helped by the willing hands of the Americans in it. He spent a very enjoyable few hours chatting to them, and when we made a brief halt to allow a train to pass us, he came running back to our box car to tell me that there were some chaps from Baltimore among his new friends. I determined to go along and meet them as soon as I could.

The train which passed us in the loop line was packed to capacity with civilians. The trucks were crammed full, and those who had not been able to get inside clung precariously to handrails, balanced on the iron rungs up the side, and even flattened themselves on the roofs, seeming to hang on by sheer will power. There were even children lying on the narrow running boards.

Jack's American friends told him that they had heard there were plenty of American transport ships in Odessa harbour. I hope they are right.

We finally pulled into a freight yard at Smerentka, or some such unpronounceable name, and stopped there until 12:30. Here the inevitable market opened up again despite the ban, and trade was brisk. Colonel Fuller hauled Jack over the coals for allowing one of our chaps to do a deal but Jack said that if the Colonel could tell him how to stop it, he would be more than happy to do so. The Germans, Jack pointed out, had been unable to stamp out dealing even at the threat of the bayonet and he was quite convinced that our chaps, hardened by five years in the prison camps, were not going to listen to any such order at this late stage. I rather think Jack retired with the moral victory.

It is different to find out just how far we are from our destination. Some say 250 others up to 400 kilometres. But I have a hunch. I remember that I was right when I predicted our move within 24 hours from Ciechocinek, and I have much the same sort of feeling that we shall be at Odessa late tomorrow or early on Friday morning. We shall see.

Thursday 15 March 1945

Continued on way today with all too frequent stops. It is staggering to see what the peasants at each wayside station produce for sale. In a country which has been under the German occupation and has had two bloody campaigns fought over it, one could hardly expect to find much food. And yet the civilians offer white bread, sugar, bacon, gherkins, fish, tobacco, cigarette papers, eggs, walnuts, prunes, milk, cheese, haricot beans, buns and oats, in abundance. And, what was even more curious, all of these items could be bought for money. In Poland it was necessary to trade goods for food, as the currency was worthless since there was nothing to buy. But here the natives are anxious to sell for roubles. Up to now, we had held out but the sight of nearly everyone else tucking in to these foodstuffs, was too much for us and two of our blankets went. Bob took charge of the money and we laid in a little stock and put the change aside against future opportunities to buy. And so we had a good tightner of one egg each, white bread and prune cakes. Boy it tasted good. [A good meaning of 'tightner' would be 'fills' or 'binds' up.]

When we had eaten, I went down the train with Jack and had a good yarn with the Baltimorean's American friends, and in particularly with the Baltimoreans. Most of them had been in the initial landings at Normandy and it was fascinating to hear their experiences. How things have changed! Most of the weapons they talk about are unknown to us. They seem to regard us with a little awe as having been prisoners since Dunkirk which has passed in history for them.

We were told officially that we are to reach Odessa tomorrow and that a telegram has been despatched to warn the authorities there of our coming. Apparently there is a ship waiting for us and we should embark almost at once. It sounds almost too good to be true.

I had a good wash and a square up this evening and turned in in high spirits.

Friday 16 March 1945

Up early to find that we are in a freight yard on the outskirts of Odessa. Orders received to clean out our trucks and prepare to leave the train. Packed by valises and then we all turned to and swept out the truck, emptied our straw mattresses and swept up. As on every important occasion on our journey, Bob put on his kilt in honour of the event of the arrival. And at 10 o'clock we piled into the train once more and started on the last four and a half miles to the docks.

But it was not the docks that we finally made for. We drew in to the main goods yards of Odessa and there were bitterly disappointed to learn that we were not to go down to the boat yet. It was a bitter blow but worse was to come. We formed up alongside the train and waited the order to march off. As we waited we were enraged to see a Russian sentry calmly pull out a packet of players and light up. And we had been given German cigars!

The inevitable counting ensued and then we marched off through the town, great objects of interest to the inhabitants, and after an hour or so arrived at a huge rambling building situated in the main square of the town.

It was then that we received the second crushing disappointment of the day. As we stood in the street waiting to enter the building, an English soldier stuck his head out of the window and greeted us. He seemed to take a morbid delight in telling us that he and two Americans had missed the boat yesterday by only fifteen minutes. It had waited two days for us and then, being so far behind schedule had to sail without us. There were, he said gloomily, no more transports in harbour. We would have to wait for the next to arrive. Spirits dropped to sub-zero.

We were billeted in the building which had once been a school. It was a vast place, some four stories high and filled with dozens of rooms and corridors. Long double sized bunks were still in course of construction, but there were enough constructed to accommodate us. There were no mattresses and we had to bed down on the bare boards.

Rumours flashed round in astounding quantities and with incredible speed: boats in, boats out, boats waiting. Most of us discounted all of them and tried to settle ourselves to wait as patiently as we possibly could.

American sailors were walking around the town, having shore leave from the freighters which were bringing munitions, supplies and equipment for the Russians. As soon as they learnt that there were British and American ex-prisoners in the building they clamoured at the gates to see us. But Russian sentries had been posted at all entrances and they were forbidden even to come up and speak to us. With typical American ingenuity however, they stood on the opposite side of the road and threw over packets of cigarettes and chewing gum until they had cleaned themselves out. Thereupon they departed with shouted promises to come up again with fresh supplies.

We were given dinner of barley stew, sauerkraut and a lump of meat. Then, late at night, we were formed up and marched through the town to a bathing centre.

There followed the familiar pandemonium of nakedness and damp heat with the usual women attendants. The baths were large and there was plenty of room for all and it was good to soak off the accumulated grime of ten days in those ghastly cattle trucks. Our clothes were taken from us and shoved into a huge delouser, so we had to sit around naked until they were done. All the time the women attendants came and went about their business and paid us no attention, but we felt like goldfish in a bowl. So much for our inherent British modesty.

Back to the billets at long last and turned in at midnight. There was no more food issued this day and our supper consisted of a slice of dry bread. And we thought to be tucking in to an English dinner on the boat by this time.

Today however, we had our first glimpse of not only a British officer but also a British woman. This afternoon an R.A.M.C Captain accompanied by a W.R.E.N.S. officer drove up to our billet in a peculiar little car which our American friends told us was a 'Jeep'. We crowded to the windows and waved and shouted to them, but they were not allowed to come and speak to us. They finally drove away again, waving goodbye and shouting out to us to be of good cheer. I can't begin to describe the feeling which rose in me, and I suppose in everyone, at the sight of our own people again.

The last thing I jotted in my diary tonight was, 'Lets get on that fucking boat.'

Saturday 17 March 1945

Arose late and to a delightful surprise of British Red Cross foodstuffs, 40 cigarettes each and a bar of chocolate. After last night's disappointments and a feeling of having been forgotten by our own people, it was wonderful to see that provision would be made for us. We had banked so heavily on being handed over to British jurisdiction and care immediately on our arrival in Odessa that it was a bitter blow to find ourselves locked up under Russian guards with no contact at all with our own people. But there was evidence that we would be looked after.

And sure enough, during the morning some representatives of the British Mission for the care of released prisoners of war arrived. There was an English woman who was a Colonel in the British Red Cross organisation, a Major in the Indian Army, an R.A.F. Sergeant and about six more British officers. These people officially registered us and gave us all the information they could with regard to current affairs, our treatment on arrival home, etc., and answered the hundred and one questions which the chaps were asking. We understand that we will get at least 42 days leave at home and that we are not eligible for service abroad again for six months after disembarkation in the United Kingdom. Jack, as senior N.C.O. in our room, was given a pamphlet to read out which told us most of the things we wanted to know. Also, and best of all, we are led to believe that we shall embark within five days' time.

Some angels of mercy, in the guise of British Red Cross girls, set up a canteen in the hall of this building and this afternoon we each got a cup of English tea and some English biscuits at teatime. Everyone's spirits are high; it is wonderful to be under the control, if indirectly, of our own people once more. I warrant that the English girls of the Red Cross, charming as they are, have never been so popular in their lives before. All the chaps crowd around them, chattering excitedly, eager just to speak to an English woman again and the girls are kindness itself in doing all they possibly can to help.

This evening there was a wonderful treat. A movie projector was set up in one of the long corridors and we saw our first moving picture show since we had left England in 1940. It was Sonja Henie and John Payne in 'Sun Valley Serenade' and it was thoroughly enjoyed by all, the Americans in particular who whistled and sang all the tunes, although they were strange ones to us, and stamped their feet in time to the music. A great evening.

Everything is happening so fast all at once that it is very difficult to try and record my feelings. Our people are so kind and patient with us that it gives us a warm glow after so much bitterness and hatred. For the first time we are beginning to feel free again and to realise that our long confinement is over. The days we dreamed of, talked of, and lived for, are close at hand now. We shall soon really be going home and shall be re-united with our people. It is a lot to take in but it is being brought home to us that we are indeed liberated, a feeling we never had as long as we were with the Russians.

The rumour today is that a ship, 'The Duchess of Bedford' is due next Saturday. Only another week.

Sunday 18 March 1945

Another issue of Red Cross today, one bar of chocolate, twenty cigarettes and some orange juice. I was one of a party selected to go down to the docks this morning to unload some barges of clothing. A Russian guard went with us as did a Sergeant from the British Mission. We did not have much work to do and had a good walk around the docks which are full of ships, mostly American. Our guard wandered off for a little while, so we seized the opportunity to walk over to the gangplank of an American Liberty ship which was tied up nearby. There was only one chap on deck but we hailed him and he came to the side and looked enquiringly at us. He did not know we were English and when we spoke to him he nearly fell overboard in surprise. We told him that there were plenty more of us back in the town, as well as some few hundred American soldiers. By this time many of his ship mates had joined him at the rail. As soon as they learned the situation they disappeared in to the ship only to reappear laden with gifts. They gave us their dinners of roast chicken, peas, and mashed potatoes followed by apple pie. We needed no urging to get it down us. When we had eaten they loaded us up with fruit, cigarettes, candies and magazines, as much as we could carry. I can find no words to express how grateful we were for their kindness. They told us if the Russians did not soon put us on board a ship, to break billets and come down and get aboard their ship. They'd look after us. What a fine bunch of chaps they were.

We loaded the bales of clothing into a truck and drove up to a warehouse in the town where we stacked them up. The Sergeant gave us some bars of chocolate and we returned to the billets to tell the chaps of our adventures. The magazines were soon spread, Broadcast being read avidly by British and American alike.

Late this afternoon I began to feel rather poorly. A heavy cold broke in my head and my chest began to become rather congested. I lay down and stayed there the rest of the day. I suppose it was all part of the reaction.

During the afternoon and again in the evening an impromptu concert was held and thoroughly enjoyed by all. A Russian officer obliged with a dance interspersed with shouts of 'Hey' and much gymnastic contortions.

I got up for my cup of tea this afternoon but went back to lay down afterwards. I only hope that I am not feeling seedy when it comes time to get aboard the boat. That would be an anti-climatic ending to our adventures.

The British Mission supplied each room with a portable gramophone today together with some records, and it is kept busy grinding out dance music and Bing Crosby.

Monday 19 March 1945

Yet more Red Cross issued today, twenty cigarettes and a bar of Rowntree's as yesterday.

My chest was really painful when I awoke, so I reported to the British Medical Officer. There was very little he could do for me, however, except to assure me that there was nothing really wrong except for a slight cold. Anyway, I felt better for his advice and words of cheer. I spent most of the day lying down and was much improved by evening.

I managed to get up and go out with the rest of the chaps when they were taken on a route march through the town for exercise. Bob wore his kilt and was the sensation of the year in all Odessa. The Russians stared at him as though he was a visitor from another planet. We marched down to the sea and it gave us all a great thrill to smell the salt air and to see the harbour. On the way back we saw a party of German prisoners being made to work clearing away bomb rubble. Poetic justice.

The Russians munificently issued us with some tobacco today, fifteen men to a packet of almost unsmokeable stuff. Another film was shown tonight: Robert Taylor in 'Song of Russia', but the sound track was so bad that we could hardly understand what was being said and I left half-way through. I went back to our room and laid down to sleep. Just as I was dozing off however, news came in of a shocking tragedy which occurred at about 10 o'clock. The wall of an adjoining bombed building, some sixty feet high, suddenly collapsed and two American soldiers who had been brewing up a pot of coffee on a little fire, were crushed and buried beneath the huge stones. They were both dead when they were dug out. Several men using a latrine further along had a narrow escape but fortunately for them only half the length of the wall fell. As it was, two British chaps were quite severely injured, although they are expected to live. This wall has never been safe, although no warning was given as to its condition by the Russian authorities and indeed we had to pass it several times daily on our way to the latrines and the cookhouse. The whole affair is rendered all the more tragic by the fact that the men had suffered and survived so much only to be killed on the eve of their departure for home.

Tuesday 20 March 1945

My chest was somewhat easier today, but my head was almost splitting open and throbbing painfully with every step I took. Felt pretty rotten and could not even cheer myself up with the thought that we would be getting on the boat for home. However, I went out on the route march again today and felt better for the exercise and fresh air.

On our return to the billets we were given an invalid Red Cross parcel each and were thus able to make ourselves some hot tea, or milk, and to have a tasty bit of creamed rice. The food put fresh heart in me and towards the end of the afternoon I began to feel more like my old self and looking forward once more to embarkation.

Today we were given a list of men who embarked on the boat which we just missed. There were 464 in all and many familiar names from Einheit Drei were among them: Winterbottom, Jimmy Hooks, Sammy Kydd and many others. I saw a C Welch and wondered if it could be Chris.

Rumour came in from American sailors that a troop transport is lying outside Odessa harbour waiting for a favourable tide to dock.

Another impromptu concert was held tonight but I did not feel up to going so stayed on my bed and looked at some

American magazines which have survived the many hands through which they have passed, but are getting pretty ragged from so much handling. I slept rather badly tonight: the billets are badly ventilated and horribly overcrowded; it gets very stuffy and smelly during the night, and bed space is extremely cramped.

The weekend, at which time rumour has it that we shall embark, does not seem to get any closer. This place is slowly but surely getting on our nerves and is proving as deadly as Ciechocinek as regards waiting.

Wednesday 21 March 1945

Head cold has somewhat cleared this morning and I felt much better. My spirits lifted in consequence, but the day dragged with nothing to do. The Russians have set up a barbers shop here in the building and borrowing some roubles from Jack, I went along to have a haircut and a shave. I can't say I was very surprised to find that the barber was a woman but it was certainly a novel experience to have my haircut and shave at the hands of a female soldier. What a queer lot these Russkies are!

The Russians were busily and belatedly engaged in pulling down what was left of the fateful wall outside our billets today. The two Americans are to be buried here in Odessa and the funeral held today. I wanted to go and managed to get myself put on the party, but at the last moment it was decided there were too many British in the party and my name was cut off along with some others. Bob Smith went however, and we all helped him to dress in his kilt. The whole funeral party had made a wonderful effort to turn out smartly and the combined Anglo-American squad looked very impressive. The whole lot of us, British and Americans gathered in the entrance hall and stood to attention while the coffins were carried through and taken outside to the waiting lorries. An American padre said a few prayers as the cortege moved off. It was a very moving and sad occasion.

The English ladies continue to serve us with two cups of tea a day and they provide a very welcome break to the dull monotony which is settling down over this place. In addition, the Russians have set up a canteen in which they sell little trinkets which some of the chaps buy as souvenirs. They started to sell some vodka but it was so potent that our British officers have forbidden anyone to buy it. Books and games are appearing in increasing numbers, but no one can settle down to enjoy them. We are all far too edgy and worked up to be still for long and most of us spend the day wandering around the building aimlessly.

The Major who is in charge of the British Mission gave a talk to the chaps today on conditions in England and at the end he answered any questions they cared to put to him. I was more disconcerted to hear V-2 bombs are still being dropped on London. I can only hope that Wembley is not in their target area.

Thursday 22 March 1945

A grey day. The only thing we had to relieve the routine of nothing to do and all day to do it in was another trip to the baths. This was scheduled for 1:30, so with typical Russian efficiency we marched off at 4:15. The water was good and hot, however, and as we have been given English soap we were able to have a really good clean up. Marched back to the billet feeling vastly refreshed and much cleaner than I had for many a long week,

In the evening yet another impromptu concert was staged and this one had more of an international flavour than the others. An American accordionist created a great hit, he certainly was very accomplished. The Russian officer who had previously favoured us with a national dance, this time did a conjuring trick which, although no one quite knew what he was trying to do, and were not much wiser when he had finished, was well received in the general atmosphere of good will.

The sensation of the evening however, was an announcement to the effect that we are to attend a circus performance tomorrow. Of all things most unlikely to happen I would have voted a circus top favourite, and this came as a complete surprise. Of all things, a circus?

Rumours fly thick and fast about ships docking and ships waiting just outside the harbour, but we are sinking in to the inevitable lethargic state which always accompanies these indefinite waits.

Friday 23 March 1945

The Russians were as good as their word and this afternoon we marched off through the town to a large building inside which the circus was to take place. It really was a great treat, and more like a normal civilian entertainment than anything we had enjoyed since leaving home. There were numerous acts: trained animals, acrobats, tight rope walkers, clowns, trapeze artists, all the paraphernalia of a real circus show. We absolutely revelled in it. Before the performance began, we were addressed by a Russian official who began his address:– 'Welcome, officers and men of the British and America armies on your way to your homes.' He got a terrific round of applause and retired highly gratified. I think the whole afternoon did more to help Anglo-American-Russian relations than anything else. It was great fun. The climax of the whole show was a very clever act entitled 'The Rocket Man', in which a man and a girl flew around and around at great speed in a captive rocket plane and performed on trapezes which swung below it.

At the end of the performance the Allied National Anthems were played and then we formed up outside and marched back to the billets. Several photographers were there and took numerous pictures which probably appeared in Russian periodicals and newspapers as evidence of the happy state of Allied ex-prisoners in Russian care.

We returned to our billets to find that our afternoon cup of tea was ready and waiting. What a wonderfully English thing this tea business is; and how miraculously such a simple thing puts fresh heart in all of us. We also received some more chocolate and cigarettes.

Later this afternoon a further four hundred British arrived and after being bathed and deloused, they congregated in the yard outside our billets for food. Having eaten they were marched off to other quarters in the town. There was only one familiar face from Thorn among them; Jimmy Woolcock who had pushed off from Ciechocinek to make his own way. It certainly didn't get him here any quicker!

This last party had an adventurous trip. The train bringing them from Lublin jumped off the rails at speed and some of the box cars were smashed. There were numerous casualties: eight dead and 32 injured. How tragic to have come so far and then to be killed on the last lap. I am not surprised the train crashed. Our own seemed in imminent danger of doing so, most of the time. Bad driving and poorly laid tracks combined to make the train journey hazardous in the extreme. It's only God's mercy that we escaped a similar accident.

Another film show tonight. It was the British picture about the adventures of the crew of a British destroyer, 'In Which We Serve'. It would have been most enjoyable but for the fact (a) The print was very old and badly worn; (b) The light in the projector was too weak to cast a clear picture; (c) A Russian sound track had been superimposed on the English so that in addition to Russian dialogue, the English was loud enough to be audible but too faint to be understood, and (d) As the film was unfurled in flash-back form, I kept losing the continuity and had soon entirely lost all track of the story. But for these little points, The Russian Cinema was a great success. I left shortly after the curtain went up!

We were just starting to get ready for some shut-eye, when we were all called out into the passages for a check roll call. Apparently some of our chaps had wearied of the Russian hospitality and had climbed out of a window and gone to have a look at the city's night life. Our hosts were dumfounded to think that such a thing could happen. Were they not doing all they could to make us happy here? Were they not kind to us and considerate? And anyway, how could the Englishmen get out when the place was guarded? We could have told them, that to men who had spent the last five years outwitting the Germans every day, getting out of this ramshackle building presented no problems. In the wee small hours the chaps climbed back through the window of an empty room and went to bed, gloriously drunk and entirely happy. Next day the Russians were amazed to find the full quota of Englishmen once more on parade.

Last rumour of the day was that the Americans are to embark tomorrow. They all seem quite definite about it; but there has been nothing said with regard to we English.

Saturday 24 March 1945

The embarkation of the Americans, which had been scheduled to take place at 10 o'clock this morning, was postponed at the last minute until later this afternoon. But as the day wore on nothing further transpired until about 3 or 4 o'clock when they were told it was no dice for today. Boy how they steamed. And who could have blamed them?

We still have had no news, although it seems fairly definite that there are two British troopships in port: 'The Duchess of Richmond' and the 'Circassia'. As proof of this we were served with English cake baked for us and sent by the crew of the 'Duchess of Richmond' at tea time. It tasted like food fit for the Gods and was doubly welcome for the kindness of the sailors who had forgone their own rations and stayed up all night baking for us.

We were dismayed to hear this afternoon that there is a great deal of controversy going on as to who is to be shipped out on these two boats. They are both British and have been sent especially for us, but the Russians are insisting that only French and Americans can go, leaving we British to wait for the next trip. We learned that a very stormy meeting had taken place between the British and the Russians at which the thing had been argued back and forth.

The senior captain of the two ships had finally delivered an ultimatum to the Russians. Either they send down the British and Americans without further delay or else he would sail out empty handed and would make the strongest protests at the highest possible levels on reaching the first British port. Later in the day we received unofficial word from the Captain. He was reported to have said, if the Russians did not take us down to the ship within the next twenty-four hours, he advised us to form up in an orderly body, march out of the billets and down to the docks and embark. He felt that the Russians would not dare use force to stop us. Once on board and technically on British soil, he would assume entire responsibility for us and would defy the Russian authorities to do anything about a fait accompli.

We were rather in a muddle about all these rumours and did not know what to do. Everyone was on edge and very nervy and the day wore on amid a welter of arguments and suggestions, none of which were very helpful. Then as evening drew in, an official Russian announcement was made. The Colonials and the Americans are warned to stand by to move off tomorrow; everyone, that is, with the exception of the British and the Canadians. This is a bitter blow to us and as we see the Americans and Colonials getting themselves ready, we cannot conceal our disappointment and frustration. It seems as if we are never to get out of this cursed place. We went to bed bewildered and dispirited.

Sunday 25 March 1945

Changes in the plans again to the changing of the Colonials. They are not to go today but are to wait behind with us. The only people to go are the Americans, some of our troops whose destination lies in the middle east, and a very small party of South Africans. They were very soon ready and paraded in the large hall of this building. As they stood waiting I contacted a chap in the South African party who lived in Durban and gave him Norman's address and asked him to let him know he had seen me and that I was in good health and on my way home. He promised to do so.

The Americans had been completely kitted out by the American military Mission here and their kit was loaded on to a truck which then drove off to the ship. The party paraded out on the main square and wonder of wonders, and to our great surprise, a Russian band appeared and took its place at the head of the column. The inevitable delays occurred, but at last all was ready. The Americans sprang to attention, the Russian military band struck up a tune which to our complete amazement we recognised as 'Roll Out the Barrel', and the whole contingent moved off and was soon out of sight, the music growing fainter and fainter until at last we could no longer hear it. The American GIs had gone.

The billets seemed dead and deserted without the lively Americans. Our chaps were cast into the uttermost depths of despair. We were only slightly cheered to hear from the British Colonel that he is trying hard as he can to get us away tomorrow. We have heard all these promises before and have reached the stage now where we will not put our faith in anything until it actually happens.

More to give us something to do than anything else, I suspect the British Mission workers took particulars of our requirements in clothing and noted down sizes, etc. This passed the time for a little while but we were soon sitting round again wondering what will be the outcome of all this waiting. During the afternoon a call was made for volunteers to go down and unload bales of clothing again. I put my name down but the job must have been cancelled for we heard nothing else about it all day,

Tonight we were supposed to have gone to see the local opera, these Russians have queer ideas of entertaining, but the jaunt was put off. Instead a few members of some Russian Operatic Society turned up at the billets and we all crowded into a large room to hear them perform. A very old and rackety piano had been dug up from somewhere and with this for accompaniment the Russians sang and danced for us for a couple of hours. The singing was not particularly first-class and no one understood a single word of it, but the performers got a good hand. There was one woman in particular, rather good looking and with a good figure which her evening dress did nothing to hide. Every time she came on all the chaps whistled, shouted, clapped and stamped their feet with approval. She thought it was all for her singing; I don't suppose it occurred to her that all of us had been shut away from the sight of attractive women for five years. She need not have done anything. The chaps would have been content had she just stood there where they could see her. But the more they whistled the more she sang and she took encore after encore. I am sure she went away with a very glowing opinion of the Englishmen's appreciation of good music.

The concert ended at about 11 o'clock. We had just crawled in to bed and were preparing to try to get to sleep when official news came in which sent spirits soaring and set everyone talking excitedly and joyfully. We are to go tomorrow. Reveille 5:30, parade 8:30, sail at 10:00 aboard the Duchess of Richmond. A terrific shout of joy went up at this announcement and the room fairly rocked with the cheering. Tongues clacked, people shouted and sang and danced around the beds. Some even started to pack their kit in readiness. Finally the lights were put out and some semblance of order restored, but none of us got much sleep. The boat had finally rolled up.

Monday 26 March 1945

We are really to go today. Its almost unbelievable, but true. The great day is here and with weather to match the occasion.

Reveille was at 5:30 and for once even I turned out in good temper. We breakfasted lightly; there was not much to eat and we could get no hot water to brew up, but none of us felt much like food anyway. We had soon finished our bits of packing and stood around in the rooms and corridors waiting for orders. Of course there was the familiar delay during which no one seemed to know what was happening and rumours flew around thicker than flies around honey.

Time wore on and the rumours had begun to take on a pessimistic tone until at about 8:30 came the order: Stand by to move off. We needed no second bidding. Shouldering our packs we filed out of the building into the morning sunshine, down the steps in to the street, and foregathered in the large square, watched by a mixture of Russian soldiers and civilians.

The Russian authorities now instituted a very thorough routine of checking. Lists had been prepared of the entire detachment and each individual name was read out by one of the officers. As a man's name was called he had to walk across the street, pass the check point and fall in in column of route behind the same Russian band which had played for the Americans yesterday. Only one name at a time was called and the Russians would not allow more than one Britisher to file past them at any given time. The next man was not called out until his predecessor had been checked, double checked, approved and had taken his place in the ranks. It was a very slow and wearisome process, but luckily there were no hitches and the column gradually lengthened while we who waited grew less and less. At long last came our names and we fell in towards the rear of the line. There were not many more and it was not long before the job was finished. Russian guards took up their places at the head, sides and tail of the long column, the band struck up a lively marching tune and in good style we sprang to attention and marched off.

It did not take long to reach the docks. As we marched through the town all the citizens stood and watched us but never proffered a single greeting or cheer. They were not the least bit interested in a batch of Englishmen on their way home; they couldn't care less. Our route took us down the slopes on which the town stood to the docks where we followed the road which ran parallel to the harbour. On we went past ruined buildings and great mountainous heaps of bomb rubble which German prisoners were busily engaged in clearing, under the watchful eyes of Red Army guards. The Jerries came in for quite a bit of sardonic jeering from our chaps, although they paid us no attention being too deeply plunged in their own miserable fate.

Just before we turned off the main road and entered the dockyard area, I was interested to see a great wide flight of steps built in to the hillside and going up and up to the very top of the high plateau where the main city stood. These I thought, must be the famed Odessan Steps on which the slaughter of the peasants and naval ratings had taken place at the time of the ill-fated 'Potemkin'.

Parker's reference to 'Potemkin' refers to a Russian naval battleship and the mutiny of its crew in 1905.

The harbour was a hive of industry. A number of ships were being unloaded of all imaginable types of war materials, tanks, guns, planes, landing strips, food, ammunition, all destined for the Eastern Front and all marked 'Made in U.S.A.' The quantity passed belief. I have never seen such a stream of equipment.

And then, as we turned a corner around some sheds, I caught my first glimpse of the red ensign flying bravely at the stern of a great liner moored alongside the quay. Here it was 'The Boat'. My heart gave a convulsive jump and I felt a warm sensation in the pit of my stomach and I choked with emotion. All the chaps were very quiet for a moment and I guessed that they were, to the last man, feeling just as I was.

We marched along the dock and came to a halt right alongside the ship that towered above us, her rails crowded with sailors and officers all shouting greetings and waving enthusiastically. The moment's emotion broke and our chaps started returning the waves and exchanging banter and wise cracks with the men on the ship. Some sailors produced large hampers of oranges and tossed them down to us and soon nearly everyone was relishing the first taste of fresh fruit for years.

As we waited the Russian band played on and on; and the Russian authorities set up another check point at the foot of the gangplank. We sprawled around and settled ourselves for another long wait. It was! Every single man was checked as he went aboard, one by one; it took ages. But again our turn finally came and we passed through. I set my foot on the gang plank, took a last look around, shook my foot to rid it of the dust of Russia and walked on board.

At the head of the gangway stood two Red Cross ladies. As we entered the ship they said, 'Welcome aboard,' and handed us a cloth bag containing shaving kit, soap, razor, chocolate, cigarettes and various other comforts. I felt all choked up again. Their spoken welcome was given to every man jack and it was said with an unmistakable warmth and genuineness which made us feel that we were truly among our own again.

We were assigned to mess decks and given a small card each designating our places in the dining saloon. Jack, Bob, Mac and I were still together. In no time at all everyone was having a wonderful time slinging hammocks and practising getting in and out and swaying wildly to and fro. I anticipate we shall get quite enough of that motion when the ship gets underway.

Dinner was served almost at once and proved to be a great surprise. I think we had all visualised tucking in to vast quantities of food without having to worry about where it was coming from. We were disconcerted to be served with a small portion of stew, bread and prunes and custard. Some harsh things were said until we realised that this was the right thing for us. Large meals of rich food after the way we had been living for so long, would inevitably have dangerous results. We are to be broken in carefully to a properly balanced diet. I got enough to satisfy my hunger, and with the thought that from now on meals would be regular, I was content.

After eating we made our way up on deck and had a good look round. Right alongside was moored the 'Circassia', our own ship is the 'Duchess of Richmond' containing British troops only. The other ship has the Americans and those Colonials who left us yesterday. We learned that we shall most likely sail tomorrow.

We were not left long to admire the view. A call went out for a working party to unload bales of clothing into a barge. I found myself being conducted down in to the innermost bowels of the holds with several others, while another party, Jack included, climbed down a ladder on to a barge moored alongside us. It was not very hard work and we took it easy. The job was soon done and we went back topside to watch Jack and his fellow workers hauled aboard again via a rope cradle on one of the ship's cranes.

By this time we were ready to eat again and were served with a wonderful tea with as much tea as we cared to drink. I enjoyed this immensely. Somehow or other Bob has become a waiter, a job at which I understand we shall have to take our turns. But we don't mind, it is such a joy to sit down to a clean table, to have all the proper knives and forks and to eat good food off clean plates and in the bright roomy dining saloon. As can be well imagined, spirits are soaring and everyone is in the greatest of good humour. 'God's in his heaven, all's right with our world.'

The crew of both ships presented a 'Welcome Aboard' concert for us tonight which, what it lacked in staging amenities, made up for more than amply in sheer good will and enthusiasm. We enjoyed it hugely.

I was dog tired. I slung my hammock, prepared the blankets according to instructions and crawled in hoping for the best. I need not have worried; I slept like a log and did not come anywhere near falling out.

Tuesday 27 March

Up early to an excellent breakfast. We spent the morning exploring the ship and having a last look at Odessa. Time passed quickly.

After lunch we gathered on deck again for word had gone round that we were to sail at 2:30. And sure enough at about that time the 'Circassia' cast off the lines which linked the two ships, drew in the connecting gangplank, and pulled out by a couple of tugs, made her way slowly seawards. We were not long in following. The Russian dock workers cast off for us and as we looked over the side we could see the gap between ship and shore slowly grow wider and wider. A Russian movie cameraman appeared on the jetty, set up his apparatus and tried to get some shots of the ship leaving. He signalled frantically for our chaps to wave happily towards the camera, but the signs they made, universal in their meaning, would not have been socially acceptable I fear. We were off. There was surprisingly little excitement among the chaps.

Later on today we were given our first pay parade and everyone received £2:0:0. The canteen was soon opened and everyone went on a glorious buying spree. How wonderful it was to spend money again. The canteen was well stocked with cigarettes, beer, biscuits, soft drinks, all manner of toilet articles, chocolate; everything we could possibly want. It was a great event.

We have been divided in to companies for the purposes of administration. In the evening a cinema show was held in the main dining hall, but our company must wait its turn for another night. All over the ship there are loud speakers over which announcements are made and radio music and the B.B.C News is broadcast. We are extremely comfortable, plenty of room, good food three times a day, cigarettes in plenty, and nothing to do except take it easy. We have lifeboat drill in the mornings and are ordered to wear our life preservers with their little red shoulder lights at all times. Three little lights designed to operate from a dry cell carried in the pocket are to show where we are in case of having to abandon ship in darkness and floating around waiting to be picked up. We have been warned not to waste the current but everyone delights in flashing them on and off at all times, 'just to see if they are still working'. We're all like kids with new toys.

Spent a quiet evening reading and strolling around the decks and then turned in to sleep well once more in my hammock. The sea is like a sheet of glass so the dining hall is filled to capacity still at each meal.

Wednesday 28 March 1945

Weather still beautiful and getting warmer. There were quite a number of things on today: lice inspection, clothing exchange, issue of kit bag, socks, towel and 80 cigarettes each. We have been issued with salt water soap for use in the showers. This afternoon I stripped and took a shower and then washed some clothing in it, lathering it well and trampling it with my feet while the hot water poured down. It was glorious and I felt really clean.

In the afternoon we reached Istanbul where we anchored to take on oil and water. Lighters and tankers moored alongside and pumped the fuel and water into our ship. The scenery is magnificent: great rolling hills and clear blue sea.

I slept for an hour or so on deck and caught the sun on my face. I am feeling and looking a little more fit now, having rested a bit. We are all impatient to get home but contain ourselves as best we can. The radio news is good and we have high hopes of an early end to the war. Berlin is crumbling before the terrific Russian onslaught and our own troops and the Americans are forging ahead like a house on fire on the Western Front. We feel that Germany cannot hold out very much longer.

This, in essence, was the end of the diary that Leonard updated on a daily basis between the dates I have included on these pages. The remainder of his diary, up to and including 21 April 1945, was made purely from memory and is not necessarily as detailed as what was recorded during the latter months of his time as a prisoner of war of the Germans, or while he was being 'cared' for by the Russians.

Although these remaining pages do not cover his time spent in captivity or as 'guest' of the Russians, I believe there is definite value in repeating them here as they help provide the complete picture of Leonard's story and are taken from what is, after all, an historic document, written by an individual who actually lived through those difficult and traumatic times.

On March 28th an order was issued by the Officer Commanding Troops on the 'Duchess of Richmond' that, in view of the danger of submarines and of information falling in to enemy hands if we are torpedoed, no one is to keep a diary and anyone in possession of a camera must hand it in to the authorities until we reach England. This is only right. Jack handed in his camera.

And so my day to day record of our adventures must of necessity come to an end. What follows I have written purely from memory and have therefore had to condense far more than I would have done if I had a written record to help me. If I have omitted any highlights I must apologise. My memory is not at all it might be. But in any case, my story is drawing to its close; there remains little to tell. We were nearly home.

Thursday 29 March 1945

The day was spent at Istanbul and it was an uneventful day. In the evening we saw a film show: 'Greenwich Village' and 'Eve of Battle,' a vivid war film which brought home to us as, probably nothing else has as yet, the stupendous achievements our forces have made, since the grim days of Dunkirk. Best of all we saw Mickey Mouse. How everyone cheered to see the antics of Donald Duck and all the other delightful Disney characters. We had almost forgotten such things existed.

The following day we said goodbye to Istanbul and pushed on once more. It was faster and we had genuine hot cross buns and coloured eggs at tea time.

Life on board the *Duchess of Richmond* must have been so different to how the men's lives had been for the five years prior to their embarkation. They were warm, had plenty of food, which included three meals a day, chocolate, cigarettes, and most importantly of all, they were finally out of danger and on their way home.

> The canteen had been selling Turkish Delight like hot cakes and everyone gorged themselves on this sticky confection. Unfortunately we began to run in to rougher waters and the ship being a shallow draft for navigation up the St Lawrence River, developed a sickening lurching motion which soon sent most of us scurrying for the nearest convenience. I decided not to wait but went to the 'doings', pushed my fingers down my throat and was deliberately and heartily sick. I felt much better afterwards and was not troubled by mal-de-mer from then on. But, oh how miserable some of the chaps looked.

Chapter Seven

The Diary of Leonard J. Parker –
Part Four: April 1945

On April 1st we reached Italy and passing the Isle of Capri, docked in the harbour at Naples. Here we stayed for six days while active troops came aboard to be taken home. There were some pretty tough eggs among them too. In particular the troops of a Canadian Mountain Regiment were some of the toughest looking chaps I think I have ever seen. What changes have been wrought since our time. In 1940 there were no such things as Mountain troops. We must seem like spectres from the past to them.

April 7th came and we sailed from Naples. As we pulled out I had a wonderful view of Mount Etna which rose in towering majesty from the sea. A truly magnificent spectacle. [The above reference should be Mount Vesuvius, as that is visible from Naples, whereas Mount Etna is on Sicily].

We had not got so much room with the additional troops on board, but we did not mind. Home was getting nearer and nearer. At Naples we had been allowed to write home and we hoped the letters would get there before we did.

Some of the chaps organised a concert. Johnny Gaskin and Wally Kersey, the only members of our Fort 13 Concert Party on board, together with Mad Maxwell, did some quite good sketches and to me seemed to be streets ahead of anyone else. But perhaps I was prejudiced.

We were now entering submarine infested waters and blackout regulations were rigidly enforced. It was strange to see the ship darkened and to have to go inside if we wanted to smoke. But I am all for it. I don't want any torpedoes hurtling through the men's deck, thank you.

I had discarded my hammock. We were far too crowded at night to sling it properly, so I slept on the table each night. In this way I avoided excessive motion too.

On April 10th we saw our first British port: Gibraltar, and we dropped anchor there for two days while a convoy was formed. We were not, of course, allowed ashore, but we could see the town quite clearly and there was always some activity of destroyers, cruisers, or aeroplanes to engage our interest. At night The Rock was completely blacked out as were all the Allied ships at anchor, but just across the way, the Spanish frontier and Spanish ships were ablaze with lights. We noticed that as soon as a Spanish ship made the slightest move, our patrol boats were out to it like a shot to see what was happening.

We had now left the fair weather behind. I suppose this was more or less fitting, since Gib was technically our first bit of England and we must have a bit of fog and drizzle to complete the picture.

The convoy was ready soon and on April 12th, escorted by destroyers, we sailed on the final leg of our long journey. We took a peculiar pride in the fact that our ship was not only the fastest and largest ship of all, but she was the flagship of the convoy. The speed was cut down, to that of the slowest ship and we did not make very good time. The destroyers scurried backwards and forwards, cutting in and out of the ships and policing the water all around us. Those who were at all superstitious were dismayed to count thirteen ships in all.

On the morning of the 13th we had gathered around one of the loudspeakers to hear the news. The announcers first words shocked us into silence and we listened with profound regret to his statement. President Franklin D Roosevelt was dead. The man who, with the possible exception of our own Mr Churchill, had done more than any one man to win this desperate struggle, had not lived to see the final fruition of his labours. The war was as good as won of course, but he had not seen the final proclamation of victory. Just as much as any soldier on the field of battle he had laid down his life for his country. Every ship in the convoy lowered its flag to half-mast and kept it thus for the remainder of the voyage. A great man had passed.

And so it was that on April 17th in the early morning, we saw the hills of Scotland rise out of the sea to greet us. We steamed in to the Firth of Clyde and dropped anchor within a few hundred yards of shore. The trip was finished and we had arrived safely home. We had taken evasive action in the St George Channel which was thick with enemy submarines; the destroyers had dropped depth charges all night long for several nights. We could hear the dull booming, clanging noise of the detonation under water as the sound waves struck our hull. It had been a nerve-racking period, but it had spelt finis to some German submarines as the patches of oil on the waters surface testified. But we had come through safely and there, within easy reach was our own land and home.

We spent one more night aboard and then at one o'clock on Wednesday 18th we quitted the ship, boarded tenders and drew away towards the shore. As we approached we could see crowds of people waiting on the jetty to greet us, when we were within a few yards, a military band struck up 'Roll Out the Barrel'. The music died away as we drew alongside and the gangplank was made fast. There was a moment's silence. No one seemed to know what to say; our chaps suddenly felt too full of emotion to move or say anything. And then suddenly the people waved and cheered and the tension was broken. In my turn I walked to the gangway, across it, then with the knowledge that this was one of the most memorable moments of my life, I put my foot on British ground.

How kind everyone was. There were civic dignitaries and military high-ups, Red Cross ladies and wives and girls from the town, all there with one thought: to welcome us home. Speeches were read and impromptu words of warm greetings spoken. They were really glad to see us. I shall never forget those good people.

We were given cigarettes galore. The train stood not a hundred yards away and we were soon installed in first class coaches for the trip down to England. The Red Cross ladies came round with papers, candles, cigarettes, cakes, and tea and pressed more on us than we could eat, drink or smoke. We didn't know how to thank them sufficiently. Perhaps they thought us unappreciative. But it wasn't that. Far from it. The plain truth is that we were overwhelmed. We could not find the words to say what was in our hearts, even as I cannot find them now, three years later. Such feelings defy description.

It is clear from the last paragraph that Leonard's recollections at the end of his diary were added some three years after he finally returned home.

The trip down was comfortable and memorable. We glued our faces eagerly to the windows and drank in everything in sight. Green fields, towns, houses, people, signs in English, all these were a sheer delight to us. At one station which we stopped at for a few minutes we spied a real live British 'Bobby' on the platform. Someone called to him and he came over smiling and asked 'What do you want, chaps?' 'Oh, we don't want anything,' said someone, 'we just wanted to look at you.' And one chap even reached out of the window and touched him a little gingerly as if he thought he might disappear in a puff of smoke.

We stopped at Newcastle and were given tea and food. And then we went on. It had been a tiring day and heads began to drop. Soon we all slept while the train thundered on through the night.

At 3 a.m we arrived at Beaconsfield, Bucks. We detrained and were given tea on the platform and then piled into trucks and drove to a camp. We were assigned to huts where we tumbled gratefully into bed and slept late.

There followed two days of re-kitting, medical inspection, pay parades and the like. I phoned home. I cannot describe how I felt when I heard my people's voices so I shan't try. Anyone can guess what it must have meant to me.

Everyone was so attentive and helpful. The telephone operator let me phone for nothing because I had no change; the local housewives gave up their time to come up to the camp to sew badges on to our new uniforms and to listen attentively to chaps who just wanted to talk and talk to women who might have been their own wives, or mothers or sweethearts. They were very understanding.

And then on April 21st Bob, Mac and I said goodbye and went our separate ways. I travelled up to London with Wally Kersey and Johnny Gaskin. For the whole journey we sat on the edges of our seats, talked nervously and smoked innumerable cigarettes.

As the train drew into Marylebone station the chaps jumped out and made a concerted rush for the barrier. I held back until the crush was over and then made my way slowly through the gate in to the main hall. At first I could not see Mother and Dad anywhere. I dumped my kit in a corner and waited a moment, and then I saw Mother running up, arms out-stretched, her eyes brimming over, followed closely by Dad reaching for his handkerchief.

Suddenly, I felt sick inside, I never felt better in my life. I was home.

A remarkable story from a young man who enlisted in the British Army at the beginning of the war to serve his King and fight for his country and protect them both from the evils of Nazi Germany. He was one of the many who survived, but only after having paid the price of being a prisoner of war of the Germans for nearly five years. He stayed strong throughout, and even when he was physically unwell, mentally he managed to remain strong and focused.

Chapter Eight

Wartime Marches

In the final few months of the War, there were a number of enforced marches across Eastern Europe of British and Allied prisoners of war, as Nazi Germany found herself on the receiving end of a committed and sustained attack by a number of units of the Soviet Red Army.

For the German authorities it was a race against time to move some 80,000 Allied prisoners of war who were being held, in camps, many of which like Stalag XXA, were situated in Northern Poland. These men needed to be moved before they were liberated and used to fight alongside the Soviet forces against Nazi Germany.

The obvious question here is why did Nazi Germany decide to move so many Allied prisoners, and endure the logistical nightmare in both manpower and food, that went with such an undertaking, when it would have been a lot easier to have simply killed them all. From an Allied perspective, it is of course good that they didn't, but it would have definitely been the easier option for them. It might well have been because of the precarious position that Germany found herself in. Not only was she being overrun by Russian forces in the east, but British and American forces were pushing her depleted forces back in to the very heartland of Germany.

By January 1945, German authorities knew full well that the war was lost, and that all they had left was to try and sue for peace. This was the main reason for trying to move British and Allied prisoners of war in to Germany. By doing so they could help protect their cities from Allied aerial bombardments, as well as using the prisoners of war as hostages, in any subsequent negotiations, as they attempted to sue for peace.

At the time, the Nazis had a total of about 250,000 Allied prisoners of war, with many of the camps they were held in, being in Germany.

Adolf Hitler issued an order on 19 July 1944, from his headquarters, at the Wolfsschanze, or the Wolf's Lair, situated some 150 kilometres west of Stalag Luft Vl, that was entitled, 'concerning preparations for the defence of the Reich'.

The camp was built in 1939 and named Stalag I-C. Initially it held Polish prisoners of war, from 1940 captured French and Belgian military personnel were also held there, and from 1941 Soviet prisoners were held there as well. In June 1943 it was renamed Stalag Luft VI and used to hold British and Canadian Air Force non-commissioned officers, and from February 1944, American airmen were also held there.

By July 1944 it housed nearly 10,000 Allied airmen. When the Russians began their advance towards Germany, Hitler gave orders to move the prisoners to other camps further west. Most of the men were moved by train to Stalag XXA, which was situated in German occupied Poland. Some 900 of these men were taken to the port of Memel, in what is now Lithuania, where they were put aboard the merchant ship *Insterburg* for a sixty-hour journey to Swinemunde, in what is now Poland. There they disembarked, with the next part of the journey being by train. The men were then force marched from Kiefheide in North Western Poland; during this march a number of them were bayoneted or shot by their German guards, before they even reached Stalag Luft lV.

As the effectiveness and speed of the Russian advance in the east became clear to Hitler, he knew that his next move was an 'all or nothing' one. He had no option but to place the entire German civilian population on a total war footing, and in doing so issued instructions for the moving of foreign slave labourers, German civilians and Allied prisoners of war in to Germany.

Hitler's order was a detailed one. Item 6(a) was the point which covered 'preparations for moving prisoners of war to the rear'. The subsequent journeys that the Allied prisoners of war had to endure, caused many of them great hardship, starvation, illness, disease and even death.

The winter of 1944/5 was severe, one of the worst there had been throughout the entire war, and nearly all of these enforced marches were undertaken by foot, with little or nothing in the way of transport or food being provided. The routes taken saw them move west through Poland, Czechoslovakia and in to Germany, and lasted between January and April 1945.

Moving 80,000 Allied prisoners of war was never going to be an easy task for the Germans, whenever it was carried out, but with a determined enemy advancing rapidly towards them in the midst of severe winter conditions, the logistics involved quickly became a nightmare. Add to this scenario hundreds of thousands of German civilian refugees, most of whom were women, children and the elderly, also attempting to make the same journey, and chaos quickly became the over-riding factor.

Allied prisoners of war that were held at Stalag Luft lV, which was situated at Gross Tychow in Pomerania, had to endure a 500-mile march, across country, in what can only be described as extreme weather conditions. On that journey an untold number of Allied prisoners perished, due to a combination of starvation, illness and hyperthermia.

Allied prisoners of war from Stalag Vlll-B began marching westward towards Germany in January 1945, as the Soviet Red Army continued their advance towards Germany. But not all of them made it. Some died from starvation, others from exhaustion, and some because of the severe winter weather conditions. It was a race against time. The German guards who accompanied the prisoners, certainly didn't want to be over run and captured by Russian forces. If they were going to be taken prisoner, they would much rather have to surrender to the Americans than the Russians.

As I mentioned in the chapter about Leonard's diary, although Allied prisoners of war were not brutalised by the Russians, they certainly appear to have spent an exceptionally long time being 'looked after' by them. But this could have been connected to outside factors, particularly in relation to 'Conferences' that were being held round that time to determine how post-war Europe was to be split up.

Just before midnight on 27 January 1945, an estimated 11,000 Allied prisoners of war, were gathered up and marched out of the main gates of Stalag Luft lll, with Soviet troops fast approaching and only some sixteen miles away. With six inches of snow on the ground and in freezing temperatures, the men were marched thirty-four miles to Bad Muskau. After resting there for more than a day, they continued their march on to Spremberg, which was a further sixteen miles away.

Stalag Luft lll was more famously known as being the camp on which the 1963 film, the Great Escape, was based. Over the evening of 24/25 March 1944, seventy-six Allied prisoners of war escaped from the camp, seventy-three of whom were recaptured, but out of these fifty were murdered by the Gestapo.

In the later stages of the war, many Allied prisoners had grave concerns about the motivation behind the Germans' reasons for moving them westward. As was commonplace in many of the camps, a rumour very quickly became the new truth. Many of them had absolutely no substance whatsoever, other than it was simply something a prisoner had thought, then verbalised his belief, which then became 'fact'.

Some of the rumours included that they were being moved towards Germany to be placed in concentration camps, where they were to be killed in revenge for German civilians having been deliberately targeted by Allied air force chiefs in aerial attacks on German cities.

It has to be remembered that 1945 saw one of the coldest winters ever recorded throughout Europe. The blizzards which swept across Eastern Europe, were accompanied by temperatures that reached as low as -13°F, and even until the middle of March, temperatures were well below 32°F. Many of the Allied prisoners of war were always going to struggle on these enforced marches, as they were ill-prepared. Many of them had been incarcerated in the German camps for nearly five years, during which time they had experienced poor rations, and were left in raggedy clothing that was in no way intended or designed for the appalling winter conditions.

Most of the camps broke their prisoners in to groups of 250 to 300 men to undertake the evacuations, but not all prisoners followed the same route. The groups would march up to twenty-five miles each day, and would then basically rest wherever they could, in a building, barn, or even under the stars. The health of these men often deteriorated due to a combination of a lack of food, exhaustion, hypothermia, and little or nothing in the way of much needed medical attention.

One rumour was that they were to be held as hostages so that the Nazis could use them as 'bargaining chips' in future 'peace deals'. At the Nuremberg war crimes trials in 1948, SS General Gottlob Berger, the General Commander of German prisoner of war camps throughout 1944, confirmed that it had been the intention to detain Allied prisoners of war in 'Alpine Fortresses'. He also outlined how Hitler had considered murdering some 35,000 PoWs unless the Allies agreed to a peace deal.

It was the Red Cross, or rather one of their delegates, Robert Schirmer, who first identified the different evacuation routes westwards that Allied prisoners of war were forced to take. The report he wrote on the subject was received by the authorities in both Washington and London on 18 February 1945.

The prisoners travelled in three different directions. First, the northern route, which Schirmer estimated was taken by somewhere in the region of 100,000 Allied prisoners; this route included those being held at Stalag XXA.

Second, there was the central route, which was centred on Stalag Luft VII, at Bankau in Silesia, which is now Poland. Those who took this route were destined for Stalag lll-A, located at Luckenwald, some fifteen miles south of Berlin.

The third route was the southern route which began at Teschen, home to Stalag Vlll-B, located quite close to the infamous Auschwitz concentration camp; the final destination for those Allied prisoners of war taking that route being the German town of Moosburg in Bavaria, and Stalag Vll-A.

Although they were referred to as 'routes', there was no exact or defined route. It was more a case of, 'there's your destination. Get there the best way that you can,' which, when taking into account that many of the marches were done on foot, was no mean achievement. Even the same routes wouldn't always be covered in exactly the same way next time around. These variations, intended or otherwise, could result in hundreds of miles being added to the distance covered

The marches began in July 1944, after Hitler had ordered all Allied prisoners of war to be moved westwards towards Germany. The first of these marches began at Stalag Luft Vl-AAX, located in Heydekrug, when thousands of Allied prisoners were marched either to Stalag Luft lV at Gross Tychow, a trek that also involved a sixty-hour journey by ship to Swinemunde, or to Stalag XXA at Thorn in Poland.

The marches threw up the most obscure dilemmas one can possibly imagine, some of which would never have been considered or thought of otherwise, mainly because the weather conditions were so severe and extreme; something most of us will never get close to having to endure.

Soldiers' boots. A fundamental piece of clothing and an everyday piece of a man's uniform. In these extreme weather conditions, a man's boots became a big problem. I would assume that to keep as warm as possible, boots would be left on, but by doing this a man risked contracting dreaded 'trench foot', more commonly associated with the trenches of the First World War. OK, let's look at the other option, 'leave them off'. If a man did this he risked getting frostbite, or his feet being swollen with the cold, or they might simply be so frozen that boots couldn't be put back on.

If all the problems and potential life-threatening ailments and conditions I have described in the pages above weren't bad enough, the last thing that most of the Allied prisoners of war would have been thinking about was the possibility of having to endure an attack from the air. On 19 April 1945, by which time Leonard Parker and his comrades were safely back home in the UK, another group of evacuated Allied prisoners of war were in the village of Gresse, which is situated in Northern Germany, when they were attacked from the air by a flight of single-seater Hawker Typhoon fighter bombers after having been mistaken as a column of retreating German soldiers; this resulted in sixty of them being killed.

Ironically, the terms of the 1929 Geneva Convention meant that Germany had a duty to remove Allied prisoners of war from a potential combat zone, as long as it did not put their lives in even greater danger by doing so. The man in charge of Germany's prisoner of war camps, General Gottlob Berger, successfully used this argument at his trial at Nuremburg in 1948. He also added that originally there was never any intention for Allied prisoners of war to be marched. The intention, he said, had always been to move them by train, but the speed of the Red Army advance took the German authorities completely by surprise. It was because of this that the incident at Gresse took place as the PoWs had to walk rather than being moved by train, as this was the only alternative.

Not all released prisoners of war were brought back to the UK by a long laborious journey by sea. On 4 May 1945, and after hostilities had come to an end, the RAF's Bomber Command implemented Operation Exodus, which saw prisoners of war being repatriated by air. The first group of 300 arrived at RAF Oakley in the early evening of 4 May 1945. Over the following twenty-three days, Operation Exodus saw 72,500 Allied prisoners of war arriving back in the UK.

By the end of the Second World War it is estimated that there had been approximately 180,000 British and Commonwealth prisoners of war held in camps throughout Germany or in territories under their occupation and control. Of these, it is believed that as many as 2,200 died, either while in captivity in one of the camps, or on one of the enforced marches mentioned above.

Chapter Nine

International Red Cross Visits – Stalag XXA

Members of the International Red Cross Society (IRCS) visited Stalag XXA on numerous occasions during the Second World War.

The first IRCS report relating to a visit to Stalag XXA by members of their organisation that I could find was dated 31 July 1940. The camp commandant at that time was Major Widmer. His aide de camp was Hauptmann Tettenborn, and a position that had the title of Homme de Confiance, which translated in to English means, 'Man of Trust', but I believe this position was actually camp interpreter or liaison officer and was carried out by Company Sergeant Major Albert Homer. The British Prisoners of War list for the Second World War records a Quarter master Sergeant Major 6908573, A. Homer of the Rifle Brigade. His prisoner of war number was 7204 and he was held at Stalag XXA.

The report showed that the camp held a total of 17,752 men, all of whom were British, except for 775 Ukranians, 262 Polish, 56 Homme de Coleur, 7 French and 3 Belgians. It was actually quite a glowing report for such a large camp, where the accommodation for the prisoners was split between wooden barracks where there were approximately 300 three-level bunk beds for the men to sleep in, tents, and the inside of the Fort.

It was noted that 187 men were recorded as being sick. Seventy of these were surgical cases, which included assessment of men with old wounds, chest infections, pulmonary congestion, some eighty cases of pneumonia, and twenty-eight cases of scabies.

The camp commandant, Major Widmer, was described in the report as being a fair man who did not like having to administer severe punishments. How that opinion was arrived at, or what it actually meant, was not clarified in the report.

One such visit took place on 13 February 1941 and was carried out by Monsieur Henri Rayet. The camp commandant was Oberatabsarzt Dr Wittkopp, and the surgeon in charge of the medical aspect of the camp was Oberarzt Dr Hoffmann.

All of the reports were written in French and were mostly routine, and included information about how many men were reported as being sick on the day of the visit by the International Red Cross Society member.

Another visit took place on 17 September 1941. Here is an extract of the report:

> Camp XIV, is the reserve camp of Stalag XXA. It is situated in part, in a Fort similar to the Forts X, XI, XIII and XV; the Fort itself is not currently in use, except for the ill, and there were only 20 sick people, who were the most seriously ill, being treated.
>
> The construction of 4 wooden huts transformed the state of the camp: the Fort in fact, was very dark and not enough light to care for the sick. It is quite different from the barracks, which are modern, well insulated and solidly built. They are divided into a large number of small rooms in which one has single metal beds or wooden bunk beds. The rooms are equipped with doormats, bedding, pillows and blankets.
>
> The camp currently has 185 beds, but this number can be raised to 330. The huts are scattered in a small wood of birch and pine, and the general look of the camp is excellent.

The report also detailed the quality and the variety of the food available to the prisoners. It mentioned clothing and said that the prisoners needed more pyjamas. It also commented on the canteen, hygiene, moral and intellectual needs, balance, personnel, post, and the sick.

Under the heading of personnel it mentioned that there were two doctors, one was British, Captain E Macral Fraser, No.1580, and the other was French, Doctor Dupont Joseph No. 1011; they were supported by thirty British orderlies. Under the heading of 'post', the report detailed that men were allowed to write and send two letters and four post cards every month, and each man received regular Red Cross parcels, at least once a week.

On the day of the visit by Dr Descoeudres of the Red Cross, he noted that there were thirty-seven prisoners with disease or injury who had been designated for repatriation by the Medical Commission, two of whom were blind with a further seven who were amputees. There were a further sixty-four men who were waiting to have their particular medical conditions reviewed by the Medical Board.

In conclusion Doctor Descoeudres wrote the following about his visit:

> Men of trust and Doctors agree that the camp is very well managed. The British and French Doctors have every possibility to treat the sick in their own time and with the agreement of the prisoners and the German authorities. Since the huts were brought in, the appearance of the camp and the conditions are greatly improved, and it is hoped that during the winter, the climate conditions will not be too rough and do not see a return of the diseases to a camp of this importance.

The obvious question that comes to mind when reading such a report is, just how accurate is it? This is not a question asked of, or aimed at, the members of the International Red Cross Society, rather it is meant for the German authorities, especially those who ran and were in charge of Stalag XXA. Were the conditions reported by Doctor Descoeudres the normal day-to-day ones experienced by the Allied prisoners who were held there, or was it all just a show put on by the camp authorities to hoodwink him and cover up any failings the camp might have been hiding?

15 May 1942 saw Doctor Schirmer of the IRCS pay a visit to Fort No.16 at the Stalag XXA camp. This was an extremely small unit which consisted of just seventy-eight non-commissioned French officers who were crammed in to just three rooms. A fourth room catered for the sick, which in effect was the infirmary and could cater for up to eighteen men at a time; there was also a fifth room, used as a library and had more than 400 books. The same fort had previously been home to a group of Russian soldiers.

The French liaison officer in the fort, Sergeant-Chef Louis Pau, who appeared to have taken his role very seriously, had demanded that the building was heated for a week so as to try and get rid of some of the dampness. The camp commandant gave his personal assurance that this would be done. This made Louis Pau very happy especially as he was already suitably impressed with the fort's sanitation system.

The next IRCS visit to Stalag XXA took place on 18 April 1943, and was conducted by Doctor Bubb and Mr E. Meyer. As a lot of these reports are repetitive in the areas they cover, I have purposely not included them all verbatim. I must point out that they were in French, but are typed, so easy to read and translate.

The report noted that discipline at the camp was strict and very severe, but the IRCS representatives recognised in their report that the camp commandant had the correct attitude and wanted above all else to prevent any escapes from the camp.

Doctor Thudichum and Mr E. Mayer, of the IRCS, carried out a further inspection at Stalag XXA prisoner of war camp at Torun in German occupied Poland, on 23 January 1944.

The report showed that there were soldiers from ten separate nations including France, Belgium, Poland, England, Australia, Canadian, New Zealand, India and America. England with 5,181, and France with 1,811, had the largest number of prisoners in the camp.

The chief medical officer was Lieutenant Colonel J.C. Mackay, and the British Liaison officer was Company Quarter Sergeant Major Reginald Granger, whose prisoner of war number was 19887. Having checked the British prisoners of war lists for the period of the Second World War, I found a record for the above man. He was serving with the Kings Royal Rifle Corps at the time of his capture, and his army service number was 6607713. It also showed that he was in camp XXA at Torun in Poland.

It was noted by the IRCS that a request had been made by the prisoners for nothing more dramatic than to ask for a quantity of ping pong balls. The downright cheek.

On a more serious note, the report also included the fact that since Stalag XXA had opened and, up to and including 31 December 1943, 121 prisoners had died. In the year 1943, fourteen British prisoners had died. Four of these had been shot, but there was no explanation as to how or why these deaths had occurred. Seven had died from diseases, one had drowned, and another had died of sunstroke.

Information about the life of prisoners of war, and the conditions which prevailed in Stalag XXA, can be readily gleamed by reading through the International Red Cross Society reports. They contain all sorts of information. Generally, life in the camp did not tend to be too harsh, which made the men's existence more bearable than could otherwise have been expected. Morale always appeared to be good among the men, for a variety of reasons. As can be seen from one of the early IRCS reports, the camp commandant seemed to be a somewhat decent man who wasn't renowned for being overly strict when it came to discipline, or that severe when it came to meting out punishments, although clearly that wasn't always the case.

The camp had a decent sized library, where the prisoners could find not only books that covered topics both of a fictional and non-fictional nature, but gave them a quiet space in which to read. Sport played its part in the form of such disciplines as gymnastics, table tennis and boxing.

Regular deliveries of Red Cross parcels were occasions eagerly anticipated by the PoWs. The parcels were always appreciated and helped the men realise that they hadn't been forgotten by their loved ones and the people of a grateful nation.

One point that wasn't included in any report that the International Red Cross Society wrote, because it was not something that they would have ever witnessed, was that of prisoner escapes. The nearest they ever got to commenting on the matter was when high-lighting the fact that the camp commandant was doing his very best to try and prevent such events from taking place.

During the war most, if not all, prisoner of war camps would have had a committee that dealt with all prisoner escapes. Any such attempts would have had to have been approved and sanctioned by that committee, which would have consisted of the camp's most senior officers or men. Such attempts needed to be part of a coordinated strategy to ensure their effectiveness, and to make sure they didn't hinder other such escape attempts. But coordinating escape attempts from Stalag XXA wasn't easy because the camp wasn't on just one site, as many of the men stayed at outlying work camps, well away from the main camp area. The other consideration was that some of the escapes were spontaneous rather than being specifically planned, and the men involved were, on many occasion, no more than opportunists. They recognised a chance to escape, and did no more than seize the moment. These men had no false IDs, no maps or money, no food, no cover story about who they were or where they were going. They survived on their wits and their gut instinct.

The most obvious danger was, of course, being discovered and shot while trying to make good their initial escape. If they made it to freedom, they then had to contemplate the possibility of getting caught because, depending on the circumstances of the capture, those discovered could well find themselves being shot by their captors, or by a firing squad once back at their camp.

Spontaneous escapes realistically had less chance of succeeding because without food and water, escapees would have to rely on locals for help, without knowing whether they could trust them or not. Depending on what route an escapee took, they could end up in one of four places: the Baltic Sea coast, Russia, Sweden or Germany.

Those known to have escaped from Stalag XXA during the course of the war are listed below. I have used two sources to compile this list of names, one of which was taken from the British Prisoners of War list for the Second World War, and the other from a well-established website. It is quite commonplace for two independent sources not to tie up, so where I have entered the words 'I could find no trace of' against names in the following list, this should not be taken to suggest there is any doubt that they had been a prisoner of war and had escaped from Torun.

> **Asprey, Private**. Having searched the British Prisoners of War list for the Second World War, I could find no trace of Asprey.
>
> **Baker, Captain**. There are 319 men with the surname Baker who are recorded on the British Prisoners list.
>
> **Beverly, Sergeant**. Having searched the British Prisoners of War list for the Second World War, I could find no trace of Beverly.
>
> **Brydson, K.J., Private** 4859162, Leicestershire Regiment. Prisoner of War number 4947.
>
> **Cook, Captain**. I could find no further information about him.
>
> **Coulthard, J.A.R., Lance Corporal** 5386215, served with the Intelligence Corps and was a prisoner of war at Stalag XXA, where his prisoner number was 5202.

STALAG XXA AND THE ENFORCED MARCH FROM POLAND

Cullen, Tom; a doctor in the Royal Air Force, who was captured in Crete by German paratroopers in May 1941, but he had been a prisoner of war for some three years before he made good his escape from Stalag XXA in 1944, along with army officer John Grieg, whose idea the escape had been.

A pre-planned 'pretend' riot distracted the camp guards long enough for Cullen and his colleague Grieg to make good their escape by walking across a frozen lake, and then scaling an 8ft-high metal fence that was topped with barbed wire. The two men had help getting to Gdansk, where they managed to get on board a ship, hide in the hold for five days, before it sailed for Sweden, a neutral country. When they arrived in Malmo they were handed over to the local police, who in turn handed them over to the British ambassador, who got them home to England.

A check of the British Prisoners of War list for the period showed forty-three men with the surname of Cullen. I was not able to trace a Dr T Cullen in the list, the only T. Cullen on that list was a Private 427466 in the Argyll and Sutherland Highlanders. I could find no such trace of John Grieg on the same list.

Curry, Captain

Foster, Frederick, Sergeant

Goodson, Captain

Granger, Company Quarter Master Sergeant

Horlock, Captain

Lathaen, Reverend

Lingane J.P., Sergeant 5384465 served in the Oxford and Buckinghamshire Light Infantry

Mackintosh, Company Sergeant Major. Other than Lingane, I was unable to find any additional information for this group of men.

Tom McGraph, Corporal was serving with the Royal Army Service Corps, who were part of the 51st Highland Division, when he was captured at St Valery-en-Caux on 12 June 1940 when General Fortune took the difficult decision to surrender.

Corporal McGraph was sent to Stalag XXA German prisoner of war camp. He eventually escaped from the camp, which was situated in northern German occupied Poland, on 9 March 1942. His was a risky escape for two reasons: first, the mode of escape; he found, or made, a hole in the camp's wire fence, and simply walked out of the camp. If he had been discovered doing so he would have been shot by the guards. Second: how he was attired. He was wearing a civilian suit of clothing. If the Germans had captured him while on the run, he would have more than likely been shot for 'being a spy'.

He had some chocolate for food and a small amount of money to help him make good his escape, which saw him catch trains from Germany to Paris in France, and from there to the Spanish border, a journey he had made using false documents which, if discovered, would have led to his arrest. He made it in to neutral Spain by walking across the Pyrenees mountain range, which separates France from Spain, and finally arrived in Gibraltar on 24 April 1943.

McLenan, Sergeant

Meatkins, Private

Robson, Private

Scotland, Private. The British Prisoners of War list shows a private 2985976 J.B. Scotland, who served with the Argyll and Sutherland Highlanders and was held at Stalag XXA. His prisoner of war number 14287.

Sivers, A.E., Regimental Sergeant Major 6337899, who served with the Queens Own Royal West Kent Regiment. His prisoner of war number was 9597. He had also been a prisoner at Stalag 383, Hofenfels, Rhineland-Palatinate.

Strawbridge, Regimental Sergeant Major

Williams, Captain

As can be seen from the above list of men, I have not been able to find out detailed information about all of them and how they escaped.

Chapter Ten

Newspaper report of PoWs at Stalag XXA

This chapter is about a selection of newspaper articles, of men of the British Army who were captured by the Germans, taken as prisoners of war and held in captivity at Stalag XXA throughout 1940. It was in the early months of that year when initial reports of British military personnel, having been captured, began filtering through among the pages of the British press.

Some of the men were single, others were married, and some of those were fathers, meaning the impact of their capture was even greater.

I do not suggest that this is a comprehensive list of those held at Stalag XXA, nor is it intended to be. It is to provide the reader with a flavour of how these men's incarceration affected their families, some of whom had to wait months for official confirmation of whether their loved one was dead, alive or missing.

1940 May

Warnaby, Ernest, Private 4392367 from Sunderland, was serving with the Green Howards in Norway when he was reported as missing in action while on active service on 28 April 1940. His wife, of 70 Tudor Grove, Humbledon, received a letter from him in May 1940, telling her that he is a prisoner of war:

> I had just about given up hope. It is so long since I had heard from him, more than a month, although I had been informed he was missing by the War Office. Now of course I am more relieved than I can say to hear that he is alive, even though he is a prisoner in enemy hands.

My husband who was employed at Hendon Paper Works, joined up on 4 November 1939, and was recalled from France before being sent to Norway. I last heard from him on 23 April after he got back from France. Now he has written to me from Stalag XXA in Germany to say he is a prisoner there. He says he is keeping well and has a little bit of work to do. He also says they are having fine weather and that he is being well treated, but he asks me to send him a parcel. He wants a shaving outfit, condensed milk, cheese, biscuits, and some cigarettes.

Private Warnaby had four young children at the time. His prisoner of war number was 4993. The British Prisoner of War lists for the Second World War record Private Warnaby as having been held at Stalag XXB at Malbork, but it is definitely one and the same man.

July

Sainsbury, Thomas and Lewis (brothers) of Hull, were both Corporals in the 15th/19th Kings Hussars, were reported as being missing in action on 18 May 1940. The brothers' parents then had to wait nearly a further two months before hearing from them in July, when they heard that they had been captured and taken as prisoners of war and were being held at Stalag XXA in Germany, although the camp was actually in German occupied Poland.

As coincidence would have it, the brothers' father, Thomas Sainsbury, a Hull docker, had fought in the First World War, been captured by the Germans and spent the rest of his time as a prisoner of war.

The British Prisoners of War list for the Second World War includes the two brothers, but it shows them both in the Reconnaissance Corps and prisoners at Stalag 383, which was situated at Hofenfels in Rhineland-Palatinate in Germany. Their PoW numbers were consecutive, Thomas was 5445, and Lewis was 5446.

Lewis, E., Private 4389093, 5th Battalion, Green Howards. On 15 July 1940, the family of Private Lewis were informed by the authorities at the Infantry Records Office in York that information had been received by the War Office that Private Lewis was alive and well and being held captive by the Germans in their prisoner of war camp at Stalag XXA at Torun. The 5th Battalion, Green Howards was a territorial unit that had been on active service in France since the beginning of the war.

Martin, W.A. Sergeant. On 24 June 1940, Mrs Martin of 30 Oriel Grove, Southdown, Bath, received a letter from the War Office in London, informing her that her husband had been, 'posted missing, date unknown, believed killed'. But on Wednesday 31 July, she literally had the shock of her life, when she received a postcard from the International Red Cross Committee in Geneva, telling her that her husband, Sergeant William Albert Martin, of the Royal Army Service Corps, was a prisoner of war, and had been interned at Stalag XXA camp, and that he was well and uninjured. 'The news has put me and our 11-year-old son on top of the world.' Mrs Martin said. 'and one of the first things we did to celebrate, was to go to the Guildhall to help the Mayoress's fund for the Spitfire.'

Sergeant Martin was a bus conductor before the war, and was on the army's supplementary reserve list, which was why he was called up as soon as the war began. He returned home on leave from France in January and again in May 1940, returning to France on 10 May, the very day that the Germans invaded the low countries.

August

McCracken, Stuart John, Private 48th Company, Auxiliary Military Pioneer Corps. At the beginning of August 1940, Mrs Stuart of 62 Anderson Street, Kelloholm, in Scotland, received information from the International Red Cross in Geneva, that her husband had been captured by the Germans and held as a prisoner of war in Stalag XXA at Torun, in German-occupied Poland.

Private Stuart had initially been reported as missing in May 1940. He had enlisted in the army in October 1939, and found himself in France as part of the British Expeditionary Force later the same month. Before enlisting in the army, Private Stuart had been employed at the Fauldhead Brickworks at Kelloholm.

At the time of his capture he was 25 years of age. The card received from the International Red Cross in Geneva, had been posted on 18 June 1940, and stated that he was keeping well.

Abraham R, Sapper 1862828, Royal Engineers. In August 1940, Mrs Abraham of 5 Shrubbery Cottages, Buckland received notification from the War Office that her husband, who had previously been reported as missing, had been confirmed as a German prisoner of war, and was being held at Stalag XXA.

Reeday, Donald H, Sergeant, Lancashire Fusiliers. In August 1940, news was received in Colne of one of the town's soldiers who had been reported as having become a prisoner of war. Mrs Reeday, who lived with her mother-in-law at 18 Parliament Street, Colne, received official information that her husband had been captured by the Germans and was incarcerated at Stalag XXA. He had initially been reported as missing. Soon after, the War Office had told Mrs Reeday that her husband was alive and where he was being held, she received a postcard from him confirming that he was a prisoner of war, that he was in good health, was being well treated, and asked to be remembered to his mother and his three children. Sergeant Reeday had been in the Duke of Wellington's Territorial Regiment, and was called up at the outbreak of war. Prior to the war he had been employed at Smith's leather works.

As part of the British Expeditionary Force, he became involved in the retreat across France, en route to Dunkirk. He and his colleagues didn't make it in time before they were captured. One of his brothers, Albert H. Reeday, who was a driver in the Royal Field Artillery, had also been part of the British Expeditionary Force, and was one of those who made it home safely. Another brother, Private Ernest Reeday, had served with the Welsh Borderers since the beginning of 1940. All three brothers survived the war.

Pattenden Aubrey Leonard, Private 6346287, Royal West Kent Regiment. The War Office notified Mr and Mrs R Pattenden of 53 St John's Hill, Sevenoaks, Kent, that their 19-year-old son had been captured by the Germans and was being held as a prisoner of war at Stalag XXA. Private Pattenden was the second son of Mr and Mrs Pattenden. Before the war he was serving an apprenticeship with Reliance Press at Sevenoaks, and in the months leading up to the outbreak of war, he had joined his local Territorial unit.

Byrne, George Henry, Sergeant 847085, Royal Artillery. At the end of August 1940, Mr and Mrs P. Byrne, of 5 Kertland Place,

Bridge Street Row, Chester, received news that their son, who had previously been reported as missing in action, had been captured by the Germans and was being held as a prisoner of war at Stalag XXA. Even though he was a sergeant, George was still only 20 years of age. He had been educated at Grosvenor St John's School, and later at the College School, Chester. Before the war, he had been studying at a college for conveyors which was connected with the Royal Artillery. He was sent out to France as part of the British Expeditionary Force in September 1939, and was reported missing in June 1940, quite possibly one of those who didn't escape at Dunkirk.

September

Bell, Jack C., Sergeant, Argyll and Sutherland Highlanders. In June 1940, Mrs Bell of 38 Maxwell Street, Dalbeattie, received a letter from the War Office in London, that her son was missing in France. For the next three months she heard nothing more from anybody. All she had was the constant uncertainty over what had happened to her son. Was he alive, had he been killed? It was a question to which she simply didn't have an answer. Not knowing whether she would ever see him again, she did what any mother would do in the circumstances, put on a brave face, smiled when she had to, and immersed herself in day-to-day life. She knew of other mothers who had lost sons, and even husbands, so she knew that feeling sorry for herself wasn't going to achieve anything.

Then, out of the blue, on Wednesday 4 September 1940 a postcard dropped through her letterbox. It was from her beloved son, Jack. He had written that he was well, and had been captured by the Germans and was now a prisoner of war at a camp named Stalag XXA. Her only worry was that he had been wounded in one of his arms, but thankfully it had only been a minor wound, and he was fully recovered.

Before the war Sergeant Bell had been working for the National Bank in Castle-Douglas, where he had been employed for over six years. He had enlisted in the Territorial Army a year before the outbreak of the war, and was one of the first to be sent out to France as part of the British Expeditionary Force.

I could only find one Sergeant Jack C Bell.

October

Skipp, W, Private 2067344, Queen's Royal Regiment (a territorial unit) had been serving in France as part of the British Expeditionary Force, and had been officially reported as missing in action since 20 May 1940. On Friday 4 October 1940, his parents, Mr and Mrs T. Skipp, who lived at Chelsea House, Wells Road, Bath, received a letter from the War Office, informing them that their son was in fact alive, after having been captured on the Western Front, and was being held as a prisoner of war by the Germans at the Stalag XXA camp at Torun in German occupied Poland.

The Skipp family had for many years lived in Canada, but had moved to Bath a couple of years prior to the outbreak of war.

November

The following letter appeared in the *Dundee Courier* newspaper on Monday 4 November 1940. It had been sent in by Mr J. Leslie Shepherd, of Inglefield, 68 Dalkeith Road, Dundee, and was dated 2 November 1940. The letter, dated 11 September 1940, had been sent to him by his son, who was a prisoner of war at Stalag XXA:

> The Red Cross have been very good to us, but we have been more lucky than most. Twenty-eight cigarettes each, one tin bully, two tins sausages between two, four 2 lb jams between eight, three tins of fruit between four, and three tins of milk, three boxes of cheese, three blocks of chocolate each. We have cocoa about nine o'clock nearly every evening. With the four of us in the same room, we had something to eat each tea time for a fortnight, and milk for three weeks. About Thursday we get our first pay. Last week we were moving huge tree trunks. It has toughened us up no end, as we had a three mile walk each way. No work this week, but we will be able to buy bread.

It was clear from the tone of the letter, which Mr Shepherd's son had written, that life for British prisoners of war at Stalag XXA wasn't so bad, but it is interesting to compare British prisoners of war in German prisoner of war camps, with German prisoners of war held in similar camps throughout the UK. German prisoners received three meals a day as well as full pay from the British government in English currency, the sums of which varied depending on their rank, and they received their pay regardless of whether they worked or not.

A check of the British Prisoners of War list records that ninety-three British servicemen with the surname of Shepherd were prisoners during the course of the war. Of these, only four were held at Stalag XXA. Private 4132221 J. Shepherd of the Cheshire Regiment. Private 5830500 R. Shepherd of the Suffolk Regiment. Driver 80370 G. Shepherd of the Royal Army Service Corps, and Gunner 764901 L.E. Shepherd.

A similar letter appeared in an edition of the *Dundee Evening Telegraph* on the same day. It was not signed, and once again it did not name the man, although he served with the Royal Army Medical Corps. The mother had sent in the contents of a letter she had received from her son, who was being held at Stalag XXA; it was dated 31 August 1940, but had only been received a couple of days before the newspaper was published:

> We are very comfortable here and tonight we've got a wireless fixed up. We have concerts regularly and they are very good. Letters are coming in and I expect to hear from you soon.
>
> I'm in with a crowd of Aberdeen boys and you should hear our plans for the future. We've even got a dinner arranged for when we get back.
>
> We have had some very good gifts from the Red Cross and they always help to cheer us up, but I'm really looking forward to a parcel from you.

December

Andrews, Edgar A., Gunner, Surrey Yeomanry. Captain and Mrs Andrews of Karamen, Walton, Surrey, received a letter in mid-December 1940, from their son which had been written and posted on 26 September 1940, 'How good of all the folk to ring up and make enquiries after me: Please give them my thanks and best wishes, and tell them I am fit and well.' He finished his letter by saying, 'Chins up, and remember, it cannot last forever.'

By the time of his capture, Private Andrews had already been recommended for gallantry.